Tales of The Awesome Foursome™:

Beatles Fans Share Their Personal Stories, Poems and Memories of The Fab Four

Volume One

Compiled and Edited by Linda Schultz

Cover drawing by
Jared Ainscough

Cover design by
Alyssa Schultz

Compilation Copyright © 2004 by Linda Schultz

ISBN 0-7414-2079-1

Published by:

INFIⓃITY
PUBLISHING.COM

1094 New Dehaven Street, Suite 100
West Conshohocken, PA 19428-2713
Info@buybooksontheweb.com
www.buybooksontheweb.com
Toll-free (877) BUY BOOK
Local Phone (610) 941-9999
Fax (610) 941-9959

Printed in the United States of America

Printed on Recycled Paper

Published August 2004

For Evan and Alyssa,
my very favorite
Beatles fans
in the whole world

Dedicated with

Real Love

to

John, Paul, George and Ringo

And to Brian,

who made it happen

Acknowledgments

With deepest gratitude to
Steve Barnes and Sharon Richards
for their suggestions and advice

With very special appreciation to
Lorrie Clark and Stephen Greenstein

With special thanks to
Susan Cohen, André Gardner,
Cassandra Oxley, Susan Ryan
and Steve Weinstock

And a big hug for Jenny

Contents

Index by Author

Introduction

The girls all wanted to marry them and the boys all wanted to be them.

Those fifteen words were the simple explanation I offered Evan and Alyssa whenever they asked me to explain the Beatles' astounding popularity among kids in the Sixties. Of course, that is a very simplistic way to describe the Beatles phenomenon. It's not exactly profound or brilliant, but it's how I've always viewed it.

In some ways, the Beatles' unprecedented popularity, influence and impact simply defy description. It is not easy to fully capture in words what the Beatles have meant to us, as they've had such a profound effect on us in so many different ways and on so many levels.

So much has been written about the Beatles and their colossal impact on music. I recall one comment that I heard a few years ago, and this essentially says it all: "There are just two types of musicians today: those who were influenced by the Beatles, and liars."

Over the years, music experts, biographers, writers, journalists, and scholars have attempted to describe and explain the unparalleled phenomenon that is the Beatles. But no one has written about the Fab Four in the unique and extraordinary ways that the writers in this book have done. This book is a collection of true stories, poems and memories straight from the hearts and souls of Beatles fans. The individual writers and their stories and poetry represent a very wide range of ages, backgrounds, experiences and emotions.

I believe that every Beatles fan has a great personal story to tell. That belief was my reason for putting together this book.

I want to sincerely thank every person who contributed to this collection. My goal while editing the book was to preserve the distinctive voice of each writer. More than anything, I wanted to capture the unique spirit of each contributor.

In 1964, when I was 13, I had a 14-year-old male penpal in California. Our correspondence had started off amiably enough. He had even sent me a photo of himself. He was a blond, California-surfer-boy type. I can't recall his name, but I clearly recall our last few angry letters. A few months after the Beatles exploded onto the scene in America, this boy wrote me a letter trashing the Beatles and predicting they would never last. His exact prediction was that in three years' time, no one would even *know* who the Beatles were. I fired back an angry letter, telling him that he was dead wrong. It continued back and forth a few more times, with him predicting, with much nastiness, that the Beatles would totally disappear from the music scene within three years, and me firing back angry rebuttals. We soon stopped corresponding.

I dedicate this book to him, wherever he is.

I am currently compiling Volume Two of "Tales of the Awesome Foursome." If you have a great Beatles story, poem or memory locked inside you, just waiting to be set free, I'd love to hear from you.

I hope that you will enjoy this trip down Penny Lane and memory lane!

Linda Schultz

E-mail: ForFabFour@aol.com

www.ForFabFour.com

All opinions expressed in this book are those of the individual writers and do not necessarily reflect the views and opinions of the editor.

To be consistent throughout the book, I have indicated the age of the writer at the time that he or she wrote the piece.

Please note that, wherever applicable, I have preserved the British and Australian spelling of certain words. These include: materialise, utilise, realise, monopolise, programme, travelled, favourite, parlour, colour, honoured, neighbours, busses, sombre, and synchronisation. This will account for alternate spellings of the same word throughout the book.

If you wish to contact me regarding this book, or if you wish to submit a story, poem, or anecdote, you may write to me at:

> Linda Schultz
> P.O. Box 1368
> Waltham, MA 02454-1368
> USA

You may e-mail me at: ForFabFour@aol.com.

Please be sure to indicate "Beatles book" in the subject line.

Web site: www.ForFabFour.com

Words are flowing out like endless
rain into a paper cup...

– Lennon/McCartney

Never Really Knew You

I have been a Beatles fan since I was about five. At this time, *The Beatles Anthology* mini-series debuted on ABC, and I watched every night of it with my mother. To this day, those nights remain some of my fondest memories.

Later on I could recognize Beatles songs on the radio, and could sing many of the words by myself. But I wasn't a true, diehard fan until the Christmas of 2001, when my parents bought me "**1**," the number-one hits collection. I was extremely fond of it and listened to it every day. I now own all of the Beatles' albums and can definitely call myself a true fan. There aren't many kids in my school who even know that Sgt. Pepper is the name of *an album*, not an officer in the Civil War. Nothing gets me more upset than to hear a kid say, "Who are the Beatles?" I get it all the time, though.

I wrote this poem one day in the summer of 2002 after watching the *Real Love* video on the *Anthology*. It makes me sad every single time, and as I was watching it one day, a very sad thought came over me: I've never lived at the same time as John Lennon. It isn't easy being a 13-year-old Beatlemaniac in the age of rap and punk rock, and this simple realization makes it even harder.

I've always found it easy to express myself through writing, and immediately picked up a pen and wrote the following poem. It made me feel just a little bit better.

Never Really Knew You

Seen you countless times
On TV and photos
Heard your voice a thousand more
But I never really knew you

Looked longingly at the places
You'd stood once before
Stared dreamily at your pictures
But I never really knew you

For you were gone
Before I came
Gone so long before
So I've never really known you

It hurts to realize, to think
That we've never lived on
This earth at one time
I will never really know you

Angelina Drummond, Age 13
New Jersey

A Sixth Grade Tale

In September 1963, I entered the sixth grade, the final year of my elementary school. The sixth grade was supposed to be "cool." When younger kids approached us (always carefully) to ask us a question, we would answer them in a cool way. The other grades looked up to us. Some younger kids were even scared of us. The teachers and principal depended on us. Despite all this reverence and adulation, I didn't have any idea how to act cool. Then one day I heard *I Want to Hold Your Hand*. The harmonies were cool. The words were cool. The music was cool. Then I saw a photo of the band. That photo was, no doubt, the coolest thing I had ever seen. I knew I'd found the meaning of "cool."

I begged my parents for Beatle boots and I begged them for a collarless sport jacket. I begged them to let me grow my hair with bangs. I got two out of three; my father said he'd kill himself before his son would go around looking like a girl.

I had lots of guy friends but I didn't have a girlfriend, and a cool guy definitely needed to have a girlfriend. It was February 1964 when that abruptly changed.

It was announced that the Beatles would make their second appearance on the Ed Sullivan Show on February 16, and this time it would be broadcast from the Deauville Hotel in Miami, Florida. "Hey," I said to my parents, "Don't Nana and Poppop (my grandparents) vacation at the Deauville? Are they there now?" My parents told me that they were indeed at the Deauville. I begged – I did a lot of begging back then – my parents to make an expensive long distance phone call to my grandparents. My grandfather and I were very close and I knew he would do just about anything for me.

Back then, we kids weren't allowed to talk on an expensive long distance call, so my mother had to make the call. When she reached Poppop at the Deauville, he asked what was wrong. My mother told him nothing was wrong but that this was a very important call, nonetheless. She explained that the Beatles – he knew about them and considered them to be filthy, loud rock and rollers – would be arriving there in a few days and that I was desperate for their autographs. Poppop asked to speak to me personally. He promised that he would do his best to get an autograph if I would promise to do my best in school. I promised.

When I told all the kids in the sixth grade that my grandparents were at the Deauville, I instantly became the king of cool. I was "the Fonz" eight full years before "the Fonz." All the cool guys suddenly wanted to hang out with me. The prettiest girls now wanted to eat lunch with me. And I knew it would all be over in an instant if my grandfather didn't come through for me.

The day the Beatles arrived at the Deauville, all my old and new friends wanted to know what was happening. I was nervous the entire day. When I got home, I waited by the phone trying to pass the time with a game of Monopoly with my mom and sister. The hours seemed endless. Each time the phone rang, I got excited and each time it wasn't Poppop. Finally! The phone rang and it was Poppop! Naturally, only my mom was allowed to talk to him.

He said the Beatles had entered the lobby of the Deauville Hotel amidst a sea of photographers, reporters and commotion. It was difficult, but Poppop managed to grab a Beatle and a Deauville Hotel memo pad. He said that this Beatle, in the midst of all this excitement and chaos, was very polite and stood there with him. Poppop asked him for *three* autographs because he needed one for each of his grandkids and didn't want to play favorites. He was surprised that this Beatle was willing to take time out and sign all three.

I stood near my mom, screaming, jumping up and down, and yelling, "Which one?? Which one??" My sister's and my favorite was Paul. Poppop paused for a moment and said slowly, "The memo pad says *Paul-something.*" We went absolutely nuts on Long Island!! Poppop asked whether he should send the autographs to us now or wait two weeks until he returned to New York. We told him to wait because they were way too valuable to send through the mail!

The autograph reads, *"Paul McCartney (Beatles)"* and it's on Deauville memo paper. I brought it to school and the girls wanted little edges of the memo paper because they would now own a shred of the paper that Paul had signed! The rest of my sixth grade year was awesome. I had three girlfriends. I played softball and football with tons of friends. I bought all the Beatles' records. But most important of all, my Poppop had come through for me.

Oh yeah, I did well in school.

Allen Strauss, Age 52
Long Island, New York

Thoughts From A Young Musician

A story about the Beatles from a young musician…

I was born twelve years after the Beatles broke up. In fact, I've never been alive at the same time as John Lennon. Yet, to this day, the Beatles remain one of my biggest musical influences, one of my biggest inspirations, and, of course, one of my favorite bands. Their music changed my life in a way that I never would have thought possible.

It started when I was born. The Beatles happened to be the favorite band of both of my parents since they were kids, and they first exposed me to the songwriting mastery of Paul McCartney, the innovation and activism of John Lennon, the quiet spirituality of the soft-spoken George Harrison, and, of course, the straightforward voice of reason, Ringo Starr. Songs like *Penny Lane*, *Drive My Car*, and *Hey Jude* became some of my first favorite songs. My parents had all the Beatles' records and a few tapes, so I got the full experience of the band's mind-bending career. For someone who rarely listened to "old" music at the time, the Beatles transcended the boundaries for me. Their catchy melodies, lush harmonies, and boundary-pushing experimentation were like nothing I had ever heard.

As I grew older and became a musician, the Beatles became a benchmark of superior songwriting and band interaction. Their songs just had this way of grabbing you and giving you a feeling you couldn't get anywhere else. I also became very interested in the genius of their producer, George Martin, who did incredible things with the limited technology they had at the time. The Beatles were a lifelong influence and had established themselves in my mind as the greatest rock and roll band of all time.

When I was sixteen, I fell into a deep depression. Typical teenage angst, really, but I just couldn't shake it, no matter how hard I tried. My days were spent coming home from school and retiring directly to my room to flop down on my bed and listen to my stereo until it was time for dinner. I couldn't find any meaning in the disconnected world around me. I was completely lost in life.

About a year later, I decided to wear headphones to bed one night after yet another sad day. Rooting through my CDs, I popped in Disc 1 of the 1967-1970 "blue album" and crawled into bed. The gentle genius of *Strawberry Fields Forever* helped me to immediately relax. And when *Penny Lane* came on, it reminded me of a specific time when I was young and an older friend had picked up a guitar and played that song for me. I smiled just thinking about it. Suddenly, with each consecutive song, I remembered different moments of my life that I associated with the Beatles, bringing on more and more smiles.

By the time the exciting riff of *Lady Madonna* kicked off, I could barely lay in my bed anymore. I had just been brought back to so many moments of my life and I saw the happiness, the sadness, the triumph, the pain, and the beauty of it all. Happiness welled inside of me and I had to stand up, knowing that the music had just triggered an epiphany, leaving me in a state of pure, excited contentment. It was incredible beyond words! And then in the next moment, *Hey Jude*, to this day one of my all-time favorite songs, graced my ears and became an anthem of the moment and of my life. I was changed forever.

The entire Beatles catalog stirs up emotions in me that no other band could ever hope to tap into. They are a musical inspiration and my life is forever changed because of their wonderful music. The band broke up twelve years before I was born. And, at age 21, I know for a fact that their impact on my life will never fade away.

Evan Brown, Age 21
Boston, Massachusetts

Beatlemania Strikes In 1979

My parents did not watch Ed Sullivan that night.

When I first learned this as a teenager, I was horrified. How could they not watch, I argued, when it was one of the most important moments in television and musical history? What could they possibly have been thinking?

"But your father didn't like Ed Sullivan!" my mother always explained, but from my teenage-angst-ridden perspective, the whole thing was unforgivable. Now that I am older, I understand. It just didn't interest them. But when I was younger, I wished with all my might that I had been born at the right time – 1950 sounded perfect – so that I could have taken part in Beatlemania. Instead, I was born in 1967 and became a delayed fan.

I discovered the Beatles in 1979, in a rather morbid way. It was during a middle school music class, when a long-haired substitute teacher, lacking any kind of lesson plan, played for us a radio program centering on the "Paul is Dead" hoax. The clues fascinated me and that weekend some friends and I pulled out their parents' Beatles LPs, playing them backwards and searching the jackets for more clues.

"There it is!" we cried, shuddering and reading the license plate on *Abbey Road*. "28 IF! 28 years if he had lived! And look! He really *is* barefoot!" Of course, we knew that Paul McCartney was alive and well. We had been hearing Wings music for years. But the mystery surrounding the hoax was compelling. Did the Beatles leave these clues on purpose? We discussed it for hours and, in the course of the weekend, made another discovery: the music was pretty good!

From that point, it seemed that I was following the same path as those girls in 1964. I had to know everything about them – that Ringo was the shortest, that Paul was left-handed (like me!), that John wrote books. I missed out on the hair and makeup preoccupations of other girls my age because I spent all my allowance on Beatles records, which were $5.99 at Kings Department Store. Instead of plastering my room with photos of Shaun Cassidy and Leif Garrett like the other girls, my walls became a huge Beatles collage.

I collected Beatle pen friends from around the world and we made little "fan books" to send around, using flowery handwriting to proclaim, "I love George!" or "Paul is the one for me!" I started a scrapbook and started cutting out everything I could find about them – reviews of Ringo's movie *Caveman*, reports of John's 40th birthday. I became a screamer and crier when my friends and I watched their movies and every week I combed the listings in *TV Guide* to see if *Help!* might be on at 3:00 a.m. (and if it was, I'd tiptoe out of my room to watch it). I played all the records constantly. I don't think I could have told you any of the lyrics to the Donna Summer or Chic songs of the time, but I knew *Please Please Me* and *Twist and Shout* by heart.

Reflecting back on my life, I'm amazed at how some of my most important memories have a Beatles backdrop. I knew how much my father cared about me when *Rolling Stone* magazine celebrated the 20th anniversary of the Beatles' arrival in America. Because I was four months short of getting my driver's license, I asked my dad to take me to the local newsstand so I could pick up that issue the day it came out. By the time he got home from work, there was a terrible snowstorm and the weather forecasters were telling everyone to stay off the roads. Still, he drove me to get the magazine.

Important people entered my life because of the Beatles. My first boyfriend and I wouldn't have connected without them. I had heard that he was a fan and called him to tell him about a John Lennon tribute on the radio that week. (I later confessed that I made that up; I was just looking for an excuse to call him!) When one of my college roommates and I were discussing whether we should live together, the Beatles became the deciding factor. "You like the Beatles? I like the Beatles, too." It was a more important consideration than having similar schedules or compatible personalities. Later, we incorporated a weekly Beatles Night in Room 916, listening to the music and playing Beatlemania trivia.

The situation hasn't changed in adulthood. I've traveled to Britain twice and hunted down important sites – the zebra crossing at Abbey Road, the Marylebone train station from *A Hard Day's Night.* I choked up when I saw their handwritten lyrics on display at the British Library. I made a friend detour to Liverpool for only one reason; in fact, when our host in Edinburgh heard of our next destination, he exclaimed, "Liverpool?! Why on earth would you want to go *there*? Oh. Wait. Don't tell me."

I raced to get the *Anthology* CDs on the days they were released. I pumped my co-workers for every detail the day that Ringo walked by my office building and I missed him. I struggled to maintain my composure at work the morning that George Harrison's death was announced. I still cut things out for my scrapbook. And I still listen to the music constantly, on CD now. I'm trying to pass the enthusiasm on to my five-year-old nephew. It's hard, but some elements are getting through. For a while, he could pick Ringo out of a Beatles lineup.

Recently, my mother took a class about the Beatles at a local college. Perhaps she thought it was time she saw what all the fuss was about. Maybe I can get her to watch the Ed Sullivan Show after all.

Joanne Mason, Age 35
Wakefield, Massachusetts

The British Invasion - A British Viewpoint

I was a schoolboy who turned twelve in 1964. I lived in a coastal resort on the Isle of Wight and, although radio was still the big thing in those days, I was getting used to being part of the first real British TV generation. There were several TV programmes we watched avidly – Juke Box Jury was one of them; Thank Your Lucky Stars was another. It was strange – I watched all the pop artists of the day (Tommy Steele, Elvis, The Everly Brothers, Cliff Richard and so on) but without any real enthusiasm. I seem to remember a sense that something really exciting was just 'round the corner, but forty years later, I can't say for sure whether this was actually so, or just my hindsight playing tricks on me.

But I do remember watching Thank Your Lucky Stars one night and loving the song *Please Please Me* – I was familiar with it from the radio – and, more than that, being struck by the look of the group. The chap standing on the left even had his guitar on the wrong way 'round! In fact, the one thing that sank the Beatles into my consciousness more than anything was that first black and white image on TV. Previous pop groups had backed a named singer, and had moved in choreographed synchronisation. But here was a group which plainly featured four distinct *individuals*. Each had his own stance, his own way of moving, all four faces were very striking, and four different and strong personalities shone through.

I am not gay – as far as I know, I have no tendencies in that direction – but I think it is not overstating the case to say that I fell in love with the Beatles at first sight. And I am still as besotted now as I was then.

Of course, that TV appearance was no more than a key to unlocking the music. We had no record player, but that hardly mattered; we had radio, and the Beatles were hardly off the airwaves for more than a few minutes in 1963. Saturday morning became the time for me to monopolise the radio for the duration of *Saturday Club* or *Pop Go the Beatles*. *From Me to You* followed *Please Please Me,* and then the monstrously effective and successful *She Loves You,* by which point the rest of Britain started to cotton on to what the youngsters had known for most of the year (and what Liverpool teens had known for some time before that).

So, in came 1964. My class at school prepared a school magazine that year, and the hot topic was, "Which do you prefer – the Beatles or the Rolling Stones?" It was not possible to like both. (One boy tried to vote for both, and he was quickly made to choose one or the other!)

The Beatles went to the States, to be met by scenes of the same sort of pandemonium that were commonplace over here. We realised, at that point, that they had found the audience they deserved: the world. Liverpool had enjoyed a much more intimate relationship with them, and perhaps it was understandable that the Cavern youngsters felt that they had lost something that belonged to them when the Beatles moved to London, but there were no similar feelings in the rest of Britain. We were glad of their worldwide success; it meant that the group and the music which I loved were guaranteed a longer "shelf life" than would otherwise have been the case. In truth, at twelve, I think I was too shallow to think any further ahead than the answers given in interviews when the Beatles were asked, "How long do you think you'll last?"

I knew they were touring, and that they were appearing at the Guildhall in Portsmouth (just across a short stretch of sea from Ryde on the island, I'll avoid the obvious pun), but my dad wouldn't let me go. I think that's the one which was postponed because Paul had 'flu.

But there was the new film to enjoy, even though it was in black and white, with a load of (but not enough!) new songs. It was good to see our boys – funny how we became so proprietorial about them so quickly, referring to them as "our boys" – giant-sized, up on the silver screen.

1964 seemed no different than 1963 or 1965 as far as we Beatles fans out in the sticks were concerned. We were greedy, greedy consumers and, no matter how much product arrived in the marketplace, we wanted more. Looking back at the Beatles' work rate in those years, particularly '63 and '64, it's a wonder they weren't burnt out – instead, it seemed to fuel them, and one of the lasting impressions of 1964 in particular was how much they seemed to be enjoying it.

At the age of 51, and living once again on the Isle of Wight, I recall what was, perhaps, the nearest miss I had with them (apart from the times I saw Paul perform live in the '70s). The big buzz in the music press in summer '69 was that they all would be taking part in a superstar jam after Bob Dylan's climactic performance at the '69 Isle of Wight Pop Festival. Well, of course, George had been staying with Dylan for several days beforehand, and John and Ringo both attended for Dylan's performance, so I was within several hundred yards of the three of them (and only a quarter of a million people between us!) But, as history knows, communication among the four of them was not great by August Bank Holiday 1969, and there was no superstar jam.

But I revisit those times, and listen to the soundtrack of my youth, often. The Beatles' music started something resonating in my soul, and it hasn't stopped yet!

Neil R. Welch, Age 51
Shanklin, Isle of Wight, UK

14

They Sang Directly To My Heart

I turned fourteen in May of 1964. In my opinion, it was the perfect age at which to experience the Beatles. I was too young to date, but not too young to dream. I was teenaged ugly, but not in my daydreams.

I suppose to those people who actually have had personal contact with any of the Fab Four, my memories are pitiful, but they're mine and they had a profound influence on my youth.

I was babysitting late one night in the fall of 1963, watching Jack Paar on TV, when he said, "Something very extraordinary is going on in England. Take a look at this!" He showed a film clip of the Beatles. I watched, and a chill went up my spine. It was amazing! These guys were different, gorgeous (despite the strange long hair) and the music was fantastic. I went to junior high that Monday and told my friends about it. But it wasn't until February 1964 that we *really* saw what this was all about!

I had to plead to be allowed to watch the Ed Sullivan Show. TV was strictly controlled by my parents and usually limited to news programs. I was enthralled, and couldn't get close enough to the screen. I remember my father sneering, "Why are you watching that with that silly smile on your face?" How could I answer? He'd never understand. I remember taking my transistor radio to my father one time while *Till There Was You* was playing, and saying, "Isn't this nice? It's a lot better than Elvis Presley!" His reply was, "At least Elvis Presley can sing." I was infuriated and insulted, but silent. He'd never understand.

My mother, on the other hand, was more tolerant. She took a carload of my friends and me to a drive-in movie to see *A Hard Day's Night* on a Friday evening in the summer. On the way there, we heard *Popsicles and Icicles* on the radio. The line, "Bright stars, and guitars, and drive-ins on Friday night" was just perfect for the occasion. Surely the Beatles would be there, watching from their own car or picking up snacks at the concession stand. (Am I the only one out there who had these romantic imaginings?)

In early September 1964, the Beatles came to Philadelphia Convention Hall. The dad of one of my friends got tickets for a group of us. It was scandalous! We paid $7 for a $5.50 ticket!! Almost forty years later, I still remember the magic of that night…standing in line on the afternoon of the concert and singing Beatle songs with tons of strangers… watching every car that passed by, because the Beatles had to get into Convention Hall somehow!

Jackie DeShannon was the warm-up, poor woman. We weren't interested in hearing her, but I do remember her being really great. I still have very fond feelings for *What The World Needs Now Is Love* because it reminds me of that night. Hi Lit, our local WIBG-AM deejay introduced them: "THE BEATLES!!!" and then there was that screaming. That wonderful screaming! I've never been able to understand or explain how we were able to hear them sing above the screaming, except that we knew the songs so well that we could tell what they were singing. I know that I didn't add to the screaming, but I just listened, not really believing what I was seeing and hearing.

Our flash pictures with the old Brownie camera didn't come out. Who knew, at age fourteen, that the flash cube wouldn't reach the distance to our guys on the stage? We were heartbroken. We had no keepsake from that night, except for the ticket stub, which I added to my scrapbook.

Years later, while I was at college, my parents moved and, without asking me, sold my Beatles scrapbook and my collection of 235 Beatles cards. I was shocked and sad, but I knew that the Beatles had done their job. They had gotten me through a very difficult and sad adolescence. They had loved me from afar and had sung their songs directly to my heart.

Sometimes I think that they actually saved my life, but I don't really know that. I do wish that I had the chance to express that sense to either Paul or Ringo. Yes, they had a massive influence on music, our culture in general, and on many generations for years to come, but do they know that they probably saved my life by giving me hope and a reason to live? If I could, I would grasp Paul's hand in both of mine and say, "Thank you. Thank you. Thank you."

Lisa Yanak, Age 53
Hatfield, Pennsylvania

Come Together

(The Quarrymen)

From Menlove Avenue,
climbing walls,
running across Strawberry Fields.

Teddy Boy artist
laughing through school,
holding a guitar:
the Gun of the working class,
melting out strings,
to a kite of anger, fury and loneliness.

A saucepan of pain,
sometimes boiling over,
spilling at the edges,
walking with an Elvis sneer and swagger.

Tea chests, broom handles,
laundry washboards,
Acoustic guitar and maybe drums.

Ducktail haircuts,
T-shirts and tight jeans,
in engineer boots.

Travelling the early days
on the One after 909,
writing songs, playing guitars,
facing each other: Mirrors
teaching songs and chords.

Connected waves of laughter
with fresh, acoustic lyrics,
bounce off silver fishes,
swimming up there.

Bubbles of possibilities bang,
shaking pillows with stretched out stories:
Golden fingers
In transparent gloves
directing traffic of a generation and more.

A. J. P. Molloy

Andrew Molloy, Age 33
Sydney, Australia

The poems by A. J. P. Molloy were previously published at
http://www.beatles.net/ a part of
http://www.AustralianMedia.com/
Reprinted with permission.

Stepping Out

Walk down eighteen stone steps:
Another world
from bustling Liverpool streets,
shadows bursting, fragments of silence
shattered in midday sun.

Through a tiny doorway to a dark dungeon,
ceiling arches over a dance floor,
connected tunnels of reddish brick
drip with sweat;
Rickety wooden chairs,
shimmering under a few token lights,
where office workers, push against girls
squashed in short skirts with beehive hair,
gulp down a lunch of imagination.

A stage: few planks on supports.
Liverpool Boys in black T-shirts,
leather trousers and jackets
spun a universe,
a left hand bass player
and right hand rhythm,
come together for vocals,
guitars spread out like wings.

A cellarful of noise:
The Cavern in Mathew Street,
sweating storms explode,
buzz and hum with Rock and Roll.

Lightning flashes
breathe out a magic
poured into bottles of youth.
Flared messages surf
from dark corners of the aquarium.

A fresh, innocent beat:
Rhythmic Revolutionaries,
step between shadows,
making their own beds:
Farmyards of Vision.

A. J. P. Molloy

Andrew Molloy, Age 33
Sydney, Australia

The Concert of A Lifetime

The date was August 21, 1965. I was fourteen. My mother dropped me and three of my friends off in downtown Minneapolis to catch a bus to Metropolitan Stadium in Bloomington, where the Beatles would be performing. With me was my first love, Jerry Shanor, who died five years later in Vietnam. My two girlfriends, Marjorie and Kelly, were also along. We all were extremely excited.

I don't remember much about that bus ride to and from the concert. What I do remember are the crowds of screaming fans everywhere. The concert was taking place in an outdoor baseball stadium. The weather was threatening. I thought we would have horrible thunderstorms and the concert would be cancelled.

Despite the threatening weather, the Fab Four made their entrance and took the stage, located in the middle of the baseball field. All the fans were screaming so loudly we could hardly hear the music. We had binoculars with us. That was the only way to see the Beatles. They all looked lovely. They were dressed in identical clothing, very neat and professional. Wish we could have heard the songs better! The Beatles had the amps turned up full blast and were shouting the lyrics into the microphones. The crowd never stopped screaming from start to finish.

At one point, I found myself down by the fence, longing to get onto the field to get a closer look at my idols. Of course, the police were strung across the barrier and no one got past them.

I'll never forget this experience as long as I live.

Shawnne McKenna, Age 52
Annandale, New Jersey

A Hard Day's Night, 1964

I was thirteen years old. The Beatles were everywhere. I had a poster on my wall. I liked John the best. There were packages of Beatles trading cards containing bubble gum, Beatles magazines, Beatles shirts, boots, pants, wigs...it was a Beatles world.

Then the movie came out. We had all seen the Elvis movies, the Cliff Richard movies. They were crummy but they had rock 'n' roll in them...sort of. The stars had been removed from their roles as rock 'n' rollers and turned into students on vacation, or roustabouts, or happy-go-lucky kids who just happened to sing. So, when they burst into song at the drop of a hat, it was just part of a long tradition of the musical.

That's the way Hollywood deals with something new...it puts it into a comfortable box with a new coat of paint. The Beatles were different. The Hollywood producers figured that the Beatles had a very short lifespan, so when it came time to make a movie they said, "Get it out fast! Make it different! And make sure you get a soundtrack!" What geniuses Walter Shenson and United Artists proved to be!

First they hired an unknown director (Richard Lester) who was American but had worked with legendary British funnymen, the Goons. Then they commissioned a script by a Welsh Liverpudlian (Alun Owen) who understood life in Liverpool, and knew the dialect and the rhythms of the Beatles' speech. They let the Beatles write all their own songs. They kept the budget tight, so they could only afford to shoot in black & white. And they allowed the Beatles to be...the Beatles. Four lads from Liverpool, who were going to London to appear on a show on the telly. It was perfect.

Until the Beatles broke in North America, I have no memory of the radio at all. My parents and grandparents listened to it. Okay, Friday night we might gather 'round to hear the Floyd Patterson/Ingmar Johansen fight. Or the World Series...sure we'd listen to that! But music? Not much, except some guys named Bobby or Frankie singing boring songs. On television it was Westerns and variety shows featuring dancing bears. The Beatles changed all that. And when *A Hard Day's Night* came out, the Beatles changed movies, too.

I remember lining up with dozens of other teenagers at the Palace Theater in Hamilton, Ontario. It was a former burlesque house, one of those big rococo places with a huge balcony and chandeliers. It was beautiful. We swarmed the place. The management, to appease the youngsters, had made it a double bill. *Lonely Boy*, a National Film Board documentary about Paul Anka, was first on the bill. It was clear that they just didn't have a clue. We laughed, heckled and jeered poor adolescent Paul Anka. Finally the lights went down again, the screen was black...and then...

CHANG!!! "It's been a hard day's night and I've been working like a dog..." Actual Beatles running down the street...falling...being chased by hysterical teenage girls...just like the girls who were screaming at the top of their lungs in the Palace Theater. Wait a minute! These weren't real Beatles...they were shadows of Beatles, images of Beatles. It was a movie. And yet the girls were screaming just as loud, on the edge of their seats, every bit as eager to see this film as they would have been had the boys themselves been on the stage. It was incredible.

I had to sit through the film twice to hear all the dialogue. The supper show was a bit quieter, but only a bit. I'll never forget this experience, and as I speak with people my age, I discover that many of them have exactly the same memory. They were different times.

The film was a tribute to the collaborative art that is film-making. Lester's avant-garde angles and quick cuts, Owens' witty script, fabulously droll performances by Victor Spinetti and Wilfrid Brambell. And the Beatles! John, Paul, Ringo and George are extraordinary. So young, fresh-faced, ready to take on the world. And the music!! Whenever I hear the music I feel like a teenager again.

A recent viewing of the film caused me to start noticing little things. Things like George Harrison with a cigarette in many scenes. John Lennon looking so vital. Ringo walking the streets, all by himself. Of course, Paul "Ever Young" McCartney. I felt a small tear in my eye. In Canada, everything is named twice, in English and in French. The French translation is "Four Boys in the Wind." How appropriate!

I am 51 years old. The Beatles are everywhere. John Lennon's *Mind Games* was re-issued on CD recently. George Harrison's last new recordings were released to great acclaim. Paul McCartney is still out there touring today! Ringo Starr is walking the streets, all by himself, somewhere (with a fine new album of his own). You can recapture the excitement; you can experience the beginning of the myth by simply watching *A Hard Day's Night*.

David Kidney, Age 51
Dundas, Ontario, Canada

David Kidney is a musician and writer. He remembers everything about the Beatles. They defined his youth. One day he saw John Lennon in a radio booth, in downtown Hamilton, on his way home from university. He has been to three different Paul McCartney concerts; saw the first Ringo Starr & His All-Starr Band tour; and took up the ukulele because George Harrison played it. He lives in Dundas, Ontario, Canada.

This article first appeared, in a slightly different format, in Green Man Review.

www.greenmanreview.com

Reprinted with permission.

Meeting The Beatles All Over Again
in
A Hard Day's Night

One of these frigid Saturdays, I'm going over to the history center in the Strip to take in its latest exhibit, the one about the Beatles. But I'm going alone. It would be a hard sell to my friends, who are all too young to care much about the Beatles. Which I should be, too. I was still listening to music boxes when they split up.

Despite that, I spent much of my adolescence being a HUGE Beatles fan. I was just discovering them in the '70s. Well, you can hardly blame me. Look at what was popular at the time. Disco.

In my prime music-obsession years, I was pining for a band that would never release another record. You baby boomers – once again, you got all the good stuff and left us busters with...The Captain and Tennille. It's not that there weren't teen idols available at the time. But Shaun Cassidy? The Bay City Rollers? Please, even as a kid I had some taste. (I confess: In my teens, I got really into Duran Duran. But only because Paul McCartney was old and married.)

Where will the current teen idols be in 15 or 20 years? If they're like the Beatles, they'll still be admired and enjoyed, even if they don't tour anymore. If they're like the BeeGees, their music will get a second surge of popularity as kind of a curio. If they're like the Bay City Rollers, no one – not even people who were alive at the time – will admit to knowing anything about them. Do you know anyone who ever bought tickets to a Bay City Rollers concert? Somebody must have.

I had Beatles posters all over my bedroom, a stack of Beatles albums that I listened to obsessively, and, in those dark days before ubiquitous VCRs, I had a constant, burning, largely unfulfilled hunger for Beatles movies. To see them walk, talk, smile, play! Wow! To see them young and wildly attractive, rather than old and hairy and strange, as they were in real life!

So when I heard that *A Hard Day's Night* was playing at the Denis in Mt. Lebanon, I had to go. Not because my adult self desperately needed to see it. I could have rented it, or I could have stayed home and had a beer and read a book. But inside me is a 12-year-old who would have been beside herself with excitement, and I wanted to take her out.

Besides, I love this movie. It's so happy. If you can watch four appealing young guys goof around, smile almost incessantly and bathe you in some of the most cheerful music ever recorded and not feel happy, your therapist deserves combat pay. I did notice things that I hadn't before. They smoke a lot, which looks kind of shocking now. And the authority figures got younger.

After the film had started, a handful of adults came in with what seemed to be an entire kindergarten class. The kids had brought lots of snacks wrapped in four or five layers of wax paper, newsprint and bubble wrap, and they talked through all the musical numbers. This kind of thing always happens to me.

I wondered what modern children must think of a band that never uses language stronger than "swine," never kisses any girls and wears ties even when relaxing. They "rebel" by going outside to run around. They play instruments and do not dance while they are singing. Oddly enough, the hysterical girls look exactly like the ones that line up for 'NSync. Except with funnier hair.

By the end of the movie, the kids weren't talking anymore. They were singing along! The audience applauded.

My inner fan was delighted. The feel-good movie of 1964 may turn out to be the feel-good movie of 2001. No f-words, no vampires, no explosions, no sex.

Very clean. And lots of fun, anyway.

Samantha Bennett
Pittsburgh, Pennsylvania
January 17, 2001

A Family Happening Regarding
The Beatles

I am an 84-year-old man who enjoys 18th and 19th century music. I have a shelf in my piano room filled with sonatas and piano renditions of operas and songs by the brilliant composers of that era: Beethoven, Bach, Schubert.

I have raised two sons, who are now adults. Both had a smattering of exposure to classical 17th and 18th century music from participating in high school bands and choruses. But they were also becoming aware and being influenced by the modern music trend of loud guitars, drums and voices – all amplified! The piercing, continuous loudness was what annoyed most parents. But a new musical age was dawning, one that was started by the Hound Dog, Elvis Presley.

My boys often talked with their friends about the current musical groups until the dazzling appearance of the Beatles on Ed Sullivan's show. This television phenomenon overshadowed other bands and performers for a long time. At the time of the Beatles' introduction in America, Christian was seven years old, and Jeff was about twelve.

One weekend in 1964, the Deep River movie house in the next town was featuring *A Hard Day's Night.* I was sure that both boys would want to see the movie. Knowing, however, that I was a purist, a classical music buff, they were not quite sure how to approach me with their request. I knew that they had completed their school work and home chores. Eventually, the two stood before me and bravely asked if they could see the movie. I would not deny them, so in a reluctant voice, I said, "Of course you can. I'll drive you there, and when the movie is finished, call me at home and I'll come pick you up."

Arriving at the movie house, I didn't even shut off the motor. I gave Jeff the money he needed, plus an extra dime (the cost of a call from a phone booth at that time) to call me when the movie was over. After watching the boys mingle and disappear into the crowd of their peers, I accelerated the car and headed home.

Before I even had a chance to sit down and put on my slippers, the telephone rang. It was my older son.

"Dad, we cannot see the movie without a parent," Jeff said. I told my wife the problem.

"Well, don't look at me!" she replied.

So I drove back to the movie house, parked the car and went into the theater to meet the boys. I bought the three tickets and sat down with them to watch the movie. When it began, I hated the ordeal, but…

…Gradually, the movie grew on me, especially the magic of the music! I noticed that the songs were actually based upon classical principles. The chords, sevenths, and modulations were balanced and easy to interpret. The antics of the fabulous boys and "the clean grandfather" were funny and interesting. We drove home talking all about the movie.

Many years later, my older son wanted to surprise my wife, my younger son, and me. We all met in Hartford and walked to the theater at Trinity College for a special showing of *A Hard Day's Night*. It was very enjoyable viewing the movie for a second time. My wife also enjoyed it.

I'd just like to add that Paul's song, *Yesterday*, is an excellent example of the Beatles' classical virtuosity!

James Lorello, Age 84
Ivoryton, Connecticut

Dream Tickets

One of my Beatle memories is as a fifteen-year-old girl travelling to the Empire Theatre in Liverpool to purchase tickets to a forthcoming appearance of the Fab Four. My friend and I arrived at Crosby bus terminus at 5 a.m. and it felt like the middle of the night, as it was pitch-black. We were dressed identically in tight black trousers and green suede jackets with a Beatle-style collarless blouse peeping through. We each had on our Beatle tights with shocking pink socks and the most pointed pair of shoes we could find!! We had our hair back, combed high on our heads.

Walking by ourselves along the dark country roads in the shadows of the trees frightened us. But we knew it would all be worth it. "If only we had tried to get in the Litherland Town Hall," my friend said, knowing we were too young.

We climbed onto the L3 bus for our eight-mile trip into town. We sat upstairs trying to see as much as we could, as we hardly ever travelled to town, maybe only at Christmas. We both grew very impatient as the bus travelled along roads we thought it could have avoided! We hoped we could get as close to the front of the queue as possible. But we were in for quite a shock as the bus turned the corner by the Empire. There were already hundreds and hundreds of Beatle fans lining the roads!

We reached the end of the queue just as it was getting light. The place was filled with screaming, chattering girls of all ages. The police arrived on horses to keep us all in order. It seemed like hours as we stood waiting to get our dream tickets to see our idols.

Finally, we were getting close. There were now only twenty people ahead of us to buy tickets. As the queue moved forward, the adrenaline rushed through my body and we hugged each other with excitement. It all had been worthwhile: begging my mother to let me go, getting out of bed in the middle of the night...that is, it was all worth it until I heard piercing screams and cries and saw girls ahead of me falling to the ground in tears. I knew at that moment that our dream tickets were all gone.

Everyone became hysterical and the police rushed forward on their horses to disperse the crowds. We cried all the way to the bus station and continued to cry all the way home! It took me a long time to get over the disappointment of it all.

The Beatles came home for their civic reception and they stood on the balcony of Liverpool Town Hall. They were my heroes and I felt proud. How they filled me with happiness, even just seeing them from a distance. The atmosphere that day was ecstatic and has never been repeated!

I never did see the Beatles play live on stage, but I have fond memories of the Cavern, where I saw many other groups who went on to find fame. I also went to George Harrison's memorial concert. Paul McCartney came on at the end to remember his mate.

These four boys certainly put Liverpool on the map and if you ever visit our city, you will see why!

Blanche Farley, Age 55
Liverpool, England

My Lifelong Beatles Journey

"But I really want that new ABBA album!" I cried. However, my aunt insisted and instead she made me get a weird-looking album by some group called the Beatles, whoever they were. The album was *Sgt. Pepper*. Quite an introduction, won't you say?

This was in 1979 – I was not quite ten years of age, and in just a few weeks I was hooked. I slowly immersed myself in the Beatles catalog. By 1980, I was a total fan – I remember being devastated when the newspaper in Bombay carried a front-page article on the assassination of John Lennon. One of my cousins in the United States sent me an iron-on sticker that said, "John Lennon 1940-1980." It became one of my favorite T-shirts.

I've listened to a lot of music since then and I've remained a steadfast Beatles fan. What amazes me about the Beatles is the simplicity, as well as the amazing multilayered texture, of their music. It's amazing how a group could achieve as much as they did in as short a time. Each album sounds different and still has that unique Beatles stamp on it.

I often ask myself what my favorite Beatles album is. It's probably *Sgt. Pepper*, as it is for many fans, but not for the same reasons. I had no idea what psychedelia was when I heard it. For me, it's simply the album I heard first and the one that got me hooked.

I came to the United States from India in 1992 with a bunch of badly-recorded Beatles tapes. I remember going to a store that had a weekend sale and spending something like two hundred bucks acquiring the entire Beatles catalog…and bought a few McCartney, Lennon and Harrison solo albums as well.

Another Beatles anecdote: a bunch of us made a trip to New York City in December 1992. We went to the top of the World Trade Center. There was a curio shop where they took photos of you and inserted them into existing photos. I had a T-shirt made of myself with the Beatles. It's a little weather-beaten, but still one of my prized possessions.

In 1999, I fulfilled the dream of a lifetime by visiting Liverpool. I took a train from London at 7 a.m. and got to Liverpool around 11 a.m. I went on a conducted bus tour called the Magical Mystery Tour. I highly recommend this. I was able to visit all the major Beatles spots. We went past the church where John and Paul met, and we saw the bank and the barber's shop on Penny Lane. We had a chance to see all their childhood homes. (Lennon's house was upper-middle class; the rest clearly had much more modest childhoods.) We saw the restored Cavern Club and, of course, Strawberry Fields. After the trip ended, I walked to The Beatles Story museum on Albert Dock – something I highly recommend. Some really nice Beatles memorabilia is on display there, including the white piano that Lennon used to compose *Imagine*.

My journey as a Beatles fan was complete in early 2002, when I got to see McCartney in concert. I had lousy, obstructed-view seats, but still it was one of the best experiences of my lifetime. Paul was in great voice that night as he belted out around 22 songs – about 17 of them from the Beatles period. He sang really moving tributes to John (*Here Today*) and George (an acoustic *Something*). My only regret is that I never got a chance to see George perform live.

It may seem odd to say this as a 34-year-old man with a Ph.D. from Harvard, but the Beatles are a huge part of who I am today. They have had a tremendous influence on me from a young age. I could find a Beatles song for every mood of mine – happy (any of their early songs); sad (*Yesterday*); wistful (*Things We Said Today, In My Life*); romantic (*It's Only Love*); and contemplative (*Across the*

Universe)…the list goes on and on. I only hope that my son turns out to be as big of a Beatles fan as I am.

I, for one, will work to make sure that he is.

Dr. Partha Mohanram, Age 34
Professor at the Business School at Columbia University
New York, New York

One Thing I Believe

And it's this.

I believe the Beatles unwittingly set us all up to believe that life would be a continuous source of intense joy and wonder. If only they could have known, could have warned us, that they were the best thing the world would ever know, that we would only have them for a very short time, and that nothing, no one, would ever compare to them. And that even if anything or anyone did, we'd be older and wouldn't feel it in the same way, in the deepest depths of our souls. We had a right to know.

When I was young, everything about John Lennon gave me hope that the future would be a good place to be, not the nightmare it had been so far, with a cold war, a sad home, and a murdered president all conspiring to cut short my childhood.

All of John's bold, irreverent comments ("cheeky" was what the press called them), the cockeyed smile that came over his face when he knew the camera was on him (even, on occasion, in mid-song), the eccentric characters he brought to life in lyrics, drawings, and stories as though they were extensions of his own oddball nature, the way he played with language as if it had no rules to speak of – it all made me feel more at home in the world than my first eight years ever had.

Even now, when I hear John's voice, I can't believe there was a time in my life when I didn't hear it. It is incomprehensible to me that I spent nine years without that sweet, peculiarly delicate voice in my head, especially since I feel that it somehow already lived in my heart.

Even now, I hear John Lennon as my mother's voice. The voice I know better than any other. The one I heard while I was being born.

Lorrie Clark, Age 48
Boxborough, Massachusetts

Visiting Abbey Road

Many a Beatle fanatic will tell you what it's like to stand outside the gates of EMI's Abbey Road Studios in London. I've stood outside those gates on just about every trip I've ever made to the UK, on a pilgrimage of sorts. I've admired the graffiti on the white walls facing the street, and took photos, of course, of friends crossing the zebra crosswalk that appears on the front of the *Abbey Road* LP and CD.

I work in the computer industry and write books, as well as play music on the side with a band called the Flying Other Brothers, who also have day jobs in the industry. Over the years we practiced enough to make professional-sounding music and eventually to perform up to eighty gigs a year. In the spring of 2001, as the computer industry took a nosedive and most of us lost our jobs, the band suddenly took on an entirely new life.

The surprise of a lifetime was our ability to book Abbey Road Studios for one night to lay down a few tracks for our first commercial CD, *52-Week High*. I approached the gates with some trepidation. I'd once been the hippie outside, sneaking around trying to add graffiti, and now I was strolling in like a conquering hero, a true musician. The receptionist greeted me warmly, as she would have greeted any band member (the previous band to walk in there had been the Small Furry Animals).

Awestruck, completely blitzed by the atmosphere, I walked down the long staircase into Studio #2 and took my place next to my fellow Flying Other Brothers. Studio #2 has many of the original Beatles recording microphones and keyboards (including the *Lady Madonna* piano and the vocal microphones used by John Lennon, one of which I used for harmonica). The music we recorded in that short session of one night was inspired, sweeter than anything we've ever done.

We recorded several overdubs for the album and were given a tour of the place, including the infamous bathroom where the Fab Four would retire for serious smoking between sessions, the cavernous Studio #1 that once hosted the orchestra for the *A Day in the Life* session, and the gold-inlaid mixing board for Pink Floyd's *Dark Side of the Moon*. The studio personnel were very friendly and experienced at giving tours. The studio takes photos of the graffiti on the outside wall every year before whitewashing the wall, and keeps the photos on a bulletin board for each year. How nice that they preserve it.

After getting drunk in the canteen and hanging out in the inner garden on the bottom floor, I realized that Abbey Road Studio was a really nice place to just hang out. Part museum and part working studio, it has hosted the cream of British rock for at least four decades. To be there and to make music there made me feel like I had attained a new level in the game of life, a level that requires new skills and offers new opportunities.

I didn't realize how much the Beatles individually had influenced my life until the passing of George Harrison, just one year after I'd visited Abbey Road. When John Lennon was killed in 1980, I was, coincidentally, deciding to change my career from corporate worker to writer and journalist. John's death had nothing to do with my decision, but John always embodied the spirit of activism, of going out and just doing it, and by reviewing his life I found the courage in myself to make the change.

While there have been many changes since then, I've had no sea change as dramatic as that one, and now this one: the one that started with my visit to Abbey Road in 2001 and is still going on as a full-time member of the Flying Other Brothers (now featuring rock legend Pete Sears on keyboards). I always thought that one had to work a day job in order to support the music habit. But, as George said in *Yellow Submarine*, "It's all in the mind."

But some of it is in Abbey Road.

Tony Bove, Age 49
Gualala, California

http://www.rockument.com/bove.html

The Beatles In My Life

The Beatles have always been a part of my life, mainly due to my mum. My mum is a huge Beatles and John Lennon fan, and, from a young age, I can recall my mum sticking on a Beatles album. It was the only music I ever enjoyed listening to.

Listening to Beatles music fascinates me because my mum has a story to tell about each song that she's playing, like, "This is where they sang to Mia Farrow's sister when they were in India" *(Dear Prudence)*. So I've always had all the Beatles knowledge around me to classify myself as a fan!

However, I never told anyone I was a fan of the Beatles. When I had no lessons at school, I'd take the opportunity to run home and stick on the *White Album* or *Revolver* to learn some more lyrics, and I'd play it until I heard a family member opening the front door.

I don't know why I never told anyone I was a fan; probably because I felt like I'd be picked on at school for liking a band that was around so many years ago. It was only about a year ago that I told anyone. I was in a class when one of my teachers asked my classmates, one by one, whom they liked to listen to. Artists like Hendrix, Stevie Wonder and the Clash were coming up quite frequently, and that encouraged me to speak up for the first time, saying I liked the Beatles – to which I was surprised to get some praise!

Not long after this event in class, some brilliant news came on the TV that Paul McCartney would be touring the UK. My parents at first just wanted to go alone, but the night before the box office opened, I left a note in their bedroom begging them to take me, and I'd even pay the £45 price for the ticket myself!

We did get to see Macca (my favourite Beatle) at Sheffield Arena on 5th April 2003, and to this day, it still feels like it was just some wonderful dream. I bought some badges from the evening, which I now have on my school tie and wear with pride!

Today, I was honoured – almost to tears – because my mum has given me some of her old LPs, some of which have drawing pin holes in them from when they were hanging on her teen bedroom wall. I'm also so happy to be able to rummage through my mum's Beatle books and magazines, watch the *Anthology* series, go on the Internet to discuss the Beatles with many other fans, get hold of their films and, of course, listen to their music.

I feel proud to belong to the same nation as the Beatles, and I feel blessed to have seen one of them in the flesh. I'm pleased the Lennon legacy is still going, as his lifelines and mine never crossed and never will. I still think of George often, remembering where I was when I heard of his passing, and being there to comfort my mum. I also enjoy seeing Ringo pop up in the news from time to time, just to see that he is well and enjoying life. He's a wonderful bloke and there should be more people like him – like *all of them!* – around in this world.

I guess I can say nothing more than, "Long live the Fab Four!"

Jessica Pickles, Age 17
Yorkshire, England

One Magical Moment

It was the day before the Ed Sullivan Show and I remember my mother being very excited about this group... telling me how big and popular they were going to be and that I needed to watch Ed Sullivan with her the following night. I remember that she showed me a picture of them in the newspaper. My reaction was, "They look like a bunch of sissies." I was planning to watch Walt Disney Sunday night.

Well, Sunday night came and I had to watch the small TV in my parents' room. My mother begged me again to come down and watch the Beatles with the family. She knew it would be a historical event. I couldn't be bothered.

I did not see the opening numbers, but when they were due to come back later on, my mother begged me one more time to come down and watch. It would only take a few minutes and then I could go back my show. I didn't want to make her feel bad, so I agreed. They came on, they played, and that was it. I became not just a Beatle fan, but a rock fan, that night.

Walt Disney lost a steady viewer that night. I had to watch Ed Sullivan every week after that, not just to see the next time the Beatles were on, but to see any other new band he might debut. It definitely was a very important day in my life and my love for the group and their music has only grown over the years.

Robert Spadafora, Age 47
Amesbury, Massachusetts

Forty Years

Where do you start to tell the story of your life when they *are* your life? When they are, quite literally, your lifeline, your joy…when you can't remember a time when they weren't there. They're your reason, some days, for getting up and continuing the grind, coping, living. (Are you laughing your ass off yet, John?)

All one has to do is conjure up their faces, turn on the music, or pop in a video and you are transported back to adolescence, when life was all ahead of you and all there was were dreams of being grown up and free and full of joy, just like *them*. They always showed us a great time, fun and excitement beyond belief, and that 'in your face' irreverence that made you double over and piss yourself. They, more than anyone, formed my personality, my perspectives and my sense of humor. You just wanted to be with them always. And I have been, every day now for forty years. Like the song describes the 'place,' "and it's my mind, and there's no time when I'm alone." (It was pretty perceptive of you for a first album effort, John.) I've often asked myself, "Am I normal?" Maybe not, but it *is* me. I have a great outlet now. I write fan fiction.

When I first set eyes on them in late 1963, I was eleven years old. By the time I sat in that very dark movie theatre in the summer of 1964 and saw *A Hard Day's Night* for the first time, John hit me like the 'fulmine.' That's Italian for 'thunderbolt' (if you know *The Godfather*, that's a very real phenomenon). They all did, really, but John was *the one*. We all have *one*. Isn't it great to have choice?

I was frozen to the spot – couldn't take my eyes off him. Even at the tender age of twelve, he was my unfolding, my sexual awakening, and my reason to laugh. Did you ever just watch him move? See his thighs planted astride that microphone, teasing the crap out of you? Don't even get me started on his voice!

Aside from the birth of my daughter, who is my best friend, my *reality* joy – no one else has come close – no one.

Look at the photos of them from 1963-1969. Can you believe the amazing changes they made in six short years? Never stopping, always moving. We could barely keep up, but we sure did try. Not to mention that they gave us the most beautiful melodies of all time.

Two are gone now, leaving behind excruciating pain and sadness beyond belief. But you know what? It doesn't really matter – *your* influence at work here, George – because they are always with me, keeping me forever young in my head and my heart. I have them whenever I need them – giving me help, love, hope and encouragement. When you think you can't take another shitty day, there they are.

Thanks, boys, for having the courage not to 'settle for the deal' like we, the masses. You will live forever in your music and our hearts and through our children, perhaps even more so than your own kids, because they knew you as mere mortals – probably sometimes as their 'pain in the ass dads.'

I'm 52 now and my mother still occasionally asks me, "When are you going to get over them?" The day after I die. And even *then,* I have visions of John waiting there for me, tapping his foot, arms crossed in front of him, saying when he sees me, "Where the fuck have *you* been?"

Lena King, Age 52
New York, New York

The Day The Music Died

I was introduced to the Beatles by my twin brother, Chris. It was around 1972 and we were twelve at the time. He had gone over to a neighbor's house. Our neighbor had a bunch of older brothers who had a collection of Sixties albums. At the time my brother and I listened to AM radio (WIBG in Philadelphia). I remember Chris coming home that day and saying I had to listen to this album. It was what has been referred to as the *Hey Jude* album. It had a bunch of reissues on it and a picture of them in a garden somewhere and Lennon had on a black, rimmed hat. It turned out that this would be the first album my brother ever purchased. (Mine was McCartney's *Ram On*.) Well, hearing the *Hey Jude* album was all it took to make us both huge Beatles fans and eventually turn our musical tastes to classic rock and FM radio.

My story now skips to 1980. I was a sophomore studying Theater at Temple University in Philadelphia. I had to take a class called "Music Appreciation" which sounds good, but actually sucked because it was all about being able to tell the difference between a concerto and a cantata, etc. Very dull stuff. One day our teacher said if we needed to bring up our grades we could do an extra credit oral report in front of the class. I certainly needed the extra boost for my grade and immediately decided to do a report on the aspects of music the Beatles had changed.

I was originally scheduled to do my report on Friday, December 5, but the person ahead of me went way too long and used up my time. My teacher said I could do it instead on the following Monday, the 8th. So, on Monday, I did my report. That night my cousin and I were at a rehearsal for a play we were in together. We left the rehearsal and hopped into his red VW Bug and took off for home.

We had gotten no more than one hundred yards when Michael Tierson, a deejay on 93.3 WMMR, came on and announced that John Lennon had been shot dead earlier that night. My cousin screeched on the brakes and we stared at each other in disbelief for a few moments. As we sat and listened to the Beatles songs playing on the radio it slowly sunk in: John Lennon was dead. My cousin dropped me off at home and all I remember was going to our family's record player and putting on the *Let It Be* album. When I heard the words in *Across the Universe*, "Nothing's gonna change my world," I put my head down and cried.

I'll always remember my next music appreciation class which was the Wednesday after Lennon's death. I was late for class. I walked into the back of the class, trying to be inconspicuous, as someone had already begun their oral report. When my teacher saw me in the back of the class, he actually stopped the class and said, "May we please have a moment of silence for John Lennon." I was stunned as the student stopped his report and the class turned to look at me. The memory is still as vivid as if it happened yesterday.

Gregory M. McPeak, Age 42
Oreland, Pennsylvania

The Night One Sweet Dream Came True

My story is not unlike those of other Beatle fans. I was ten years old when the Beatles came to America in 1964. I was a 'young' ten, meaning I was still more childlike than preteen. Anyway, all that changed on February 9, 1964, after the Ed Sullivan Show.

I remember everyone buzzing about the show at school the next day. To be honest, I had not heard anything about the Beatles until I saw them on the Sullivan show. But, of course, after seeing that first appearance, I was a total Beatlemaniac. I couldn't get enough of them. We screamed when we heard their songs on the radio. We held our breath when an interview was given airplay. (I remember that it was very hard for us to understand their accents, but we strained to take in every word.)

One of my most vivid memories of that year was of standing in line at the Broadway movie theater in South Philadelphia waiting to get in to see *A Hard Day's Night*. We lined up several hours before they would even let us in. The girls were all screaming; a few even fainted. The theater's manager held a megaphone and screamed into it that if we didn't calm down, he wasn't going to let us into the theater. He should have known that the crowd would have attacked him had he denied us entry.

Finally, we got in and the screaming just became more intense (and the movie hadn't even started). When it did begin, the crowd went crazy – everyone screamed non-stop throughout the entire movie, myself included. I don't think I heard the actual dialogue of the movie until I saw it for the fifth time. By then the screaming was limited to the song parts of the movie – I guess the others wanted to hear the dialogue too, so the crowd finally settled down a bit after four or five screenings of the film.

This behavior continued for me personally for quite some time (through the rest of 1964 and most of 1965). By 1966, the Beatles' music began to evolve dramatically and I admit that they were progressing further than my twelve-year-old mind could comprehend. This was the time when the Monkees were coming of age and, for a time, my devotion shifted to that group because they better suited my teenybopper mentality. The Beatles actually lost some of their young fans during this period. When *Strawberry Fields Forever* was released in early '67, I remember seeing the film on American Bandstand. When they showed the reaction of the audience, you could see that most of the teenagers didn't get it either. Just goes to prove that the Beatles were indeed trendsetters and way ahead of their time.

Happily, I came to my senses in the fall of 1968 when I was a sophomore in high school. This was when *Hey Jude* was released. I remember seeing the video on the Smothers Brothers Show – I even remember the date – October 6, 1968. I remember it because I saw Paul singing and it was like seeing him for the first time. I know it sounds corny, but it's true.

After that, I really couldn't get enough of Paul and the Beatles. I went out and bought every album that I didn't have, which was most of them. I recall getting the *White Album* and playing it over and over – as soon as I'd get home from school, my best buddy at the time and I would retreat to my room and play it (forward and backward) and dissect every part of it. That was such a fun time for me.

Then, in March of '69 – horror of horrors! – Paul married Linda! Who was this American divorcée who so boldly married our Paul! The hallways of my high school were filled with crying teens, myself included. My memory of this day is very vivid.

October '69 brings another cause for crying: the "Paul is Dead" rumor surfaces. We were completely freaked out by this news. Even after the initial story broke and it was confirmed that indeed Paul was alive and well, many of us kept thinking, *what if it is really true?* That story caused much speculation for quite some time. Finally, though, I was convinced that Paul was very much alive and well.

Of course, not long after this, in April 1970, came the devastating announcement that the Beatles were no more. I won't go into detail about the state of depression that I and many other fans were in following that announcement – that, too, has been well-documented.

The next event was a happier one: the premiere of *Let It Be*. I had won the tickets on the radio, and a friend and I cut school that day to attend. Even though it was not well-received by the critics, and it is well-known that the Beatles were constantly fighting with each other during this period, I *loved* this movie. I must have seen it twenty times during the rest of that year. I suppose the fact that so much of it focused on Paul was all I really cared about.

Now, as time went on, I did mature (just a little) and wasn't as fanatical about the Beatles as I had been as a teenager. But I still loved them and bought all their solo material in the '70s and '80s. I saw Paul when he came to the Spectrum in Philadelphia in 1976. I couldn't let on to my date how much I adored Paul, but it was so wonderful to finally see him in person (albeit at a distance). I saw Paul again on his World Tour in 1990, this time with my husband, who knows all about my love for Paul and the Beatles and who just accepts it like a good husband should. That, too, was a wonderful experience, but…

My big moment arrived on the evening of June 13, 1993. By some act of divine intervention, I managed to get a front row seat to see Paul perform at Veterans Stadium. It was a beautiful Sunday and our local radio station was celebrating by playing all Beatles all day. I was in a complete state of euphoria that whole day, just thinking about my big chance to see Paul up close and personal. I was not disappointed.

When I arrived at the stadium (probably two hours before the concert because I wanted to take in all the pre-show excitement) I parted company with my husband at the gate (he had a seat upstairs) and began this great adventure.

As I proceeded down the very long aisle to the front row, I showed my ticket to every usher I passed. I needed to hear every one of them say, "Keep going – it's all the way down front." When I did get to the front, I found that my seat was one seat off center – could I be dreaming? After getting acquainted with the woman seated next to me – whom I decided I would latch onto and share this momentous occasion with – I prepared for the big moment.

After what seemed like forever, darkness descended on the stadium and you could feel the tension rise. I had such a lump in my throat already; I just hoped I wouldn't faint when Paul came out on stage. Between where I was seated and the stage, there was about an eight-foot gap that was a sort of "protected area" around which guards were standing. As soon as the twelve-minute film began (anyone who saw that tour will remember the film), the guards parted and let the fans congregate at the foot of the stage. Of course, I moved up immediately upon seeing the parting of the guards and now I'm standing right at the foot of the stage. I kept asking myself, "Can this be for real??"

Then the moment finally arrived! The film was over and the crowd was screaming and out onto the stage walked Paul. It was like being fourteen all over again. I screamed and cried and it was WONDERFUL!!! After 25 years, my dream had come true. There he was, standing right in front of me. I could see him with my own eyes and he was every bit as gorgeous as I knew he would be. Every song he sang brought out a different emotion. So many of them took me right back to remembering the first time I'd heard them.

Here was the absolutely best thing, though! As the rest of the audience was in darkness, the small gap between the stage and seats was well-lit, so the fifty of us in the front were the only ones that Paul could actually see. It was as if he performed a private concert just for us. He makes unbelievable eye contact with his audience. The woman next to me with whom I had become friendly had a large British flag that she would wave to get his attention, so he looked our way quite a bit. The absolute *best*, though, was when he looked at her and then looked down the row directly at me. That was when I completely lost it. Even though it was probably for just about one second, that direct eye contact with him is something which I WILL NEVER FORGET. I still get chills just thinking about it.

This was such an incredible evening that when the last encore was over and Paul and the band left the stage, I just stood there for about twenty minutes. I could not even move. I didn't want it to end. I know it sounds sophomoric for a grown woman to have this reaction, but this was 25 years of pent-up desire to see someone that I held in such high esteem for all that time.

When I finally made my way out of the stadium and met up with my husband, he knew that I would be a mess, and I was. I couldn't speak; all I could do was cry. It was such a completely emotionally-draining experience for me and one that I feel so lucky to have happen to me.

I've seen Paul perform once more since then, in April 2002, and it, too, was wonderful. But nothing will ever compare with the experience of having that front row seat, of watching Paul perform for two and a half hours right in front of me, and of that one amazing second of eye contact with him.

Lena Marroletti, Age 50
Turnersville, New Jersey

The Long Ride Home

I was eleven years old in July 1985. My family was living at our New Jersey seashore home. In those days it was uncommon to have a telephone in a summer home and we were no different. One day a police officer appeared at our door. He told us to telephone a relative who then gave us the sad news that my maternal grandmother had passed away.

I made the long trip back to our Pennsylvania home with my mother. I don't think we spoke ten words the whole ride home as we quietly pondered the days of mourning ahead and let the radio fill the uncomfortable silence. At some point in the journey the deejay cued up *Let It Be*. For eternity that song will always remind me of my grandmother. It evokes happy, comforting memories of a difficult day. Dozens of songs filled that ride, but I only remember hearing *Let It Be*.

I never knew my grandmother very well. As I was very young and we only saw her on holidays when my very large family gathered, I have very few memories of interacting with her beyond "hello" and "goodbye." The lads from Liverpool have given those missing memories a song that will always bring her to mind.

The Beatles' ability to move people through their music is epitomized in the experience I shared on that July day. That they continue to do so four decades after they first arrived in America is a testament to how truly great and unique they are. Their music can envelop you in comfort, move you to tears at the memories it evokes, or simply make you feel better.

Brian Miles, Age 30
Blue Bell, Pennsylvania

The Beatles And Me

As a child born in '61, I wasn't really aware of the Beatles. My parents were mainly into 1940s swing, and in my mum's case, Frank Sinatra. In fact, I don't remember us owning a record player until around 1970-71, when I suddenly became aware of Donny Osmond and his not-so-good-looking brothers.

I suppose I must have known about Beatles music, but as I went through my teens (and with them, the Bay City Rollers), Beatles music didn't have an impact on my life.

In my late teens my musical tastes changed and I became aware of early Genesis and eventually, the Beatles. The latter really came into my life through Steve (my now ex-husband) who was, and still is, a massive fan. He was the one who taught me to love their music.

At around the same time I learnt what the Beatles meant to those around me, when, on that fateful day in 1980, I arrived at work to find a male colleague in tears. Believing him to have had yet another argument with his wife, I didn't take much notice until I heard him say, "But he's been shot!" and that's when I realised John had been taken from us.

I remember my first trip to Liverpool to 'do' the Beatles bit as being completely wonderful. On the Magical Mystery Tour bus we stopped outside each of their houses. I can remember thinking how foreboding Menlove Avenue seemed to be. Having now been inside Mendips, I still think it is a bit sombre, but it is still a special place, and obviously meant a great deal to John.

Holidays over the last twenty-plus years have invariably involved a Beatle connection – Candlestick Park (to see the 49'ers play) and the Cow Palace in San Francisco, and even this year, when I went to Shea Stadium in New

York to see Bruce Springsteen. As I watched Bruce, my hero, play that arena, I kept imagining what it must have been like to have been a teenager in the '60s and have seen the Beatles perform there.

The first time I saw *Imagine* was in a cinema in Nottingham with only three other people – and this year, *The Concert for George* with hardly more than three others in attendance – but these are always special memories for me.

The annual Beatle Weeks in Liverpool have always been wonderful events and have brought me lots of wonderful new friends – Jackie in Inverness and Marcus in Huddersfield, to name just two. The year 2003 took me to the wonderful city of Boston to attend The Fest for Beatles Fans, giving me the opportunity to meet new Beatle friends and share my memories of the group.

I have seen many "supergroups" and "superstars," but how I often wish that I had been born ten years earlier so I could've lived through Beatlemania!

The Beatles have touched my life in many places, and there will always be a part of them and their music with me. No matter what happens in the world and to me, their music will always be special.

Yvonne Shephard, Age 43
Stafford, England

Hanging With The Beatles

I would love to share my stories and memories of the Beatles in Hamburg in '61, or hanging with the Beatles in New York City in '64, but those memories remain the realm of fiction and fantasy alone.

I was an eight-year-old kid in Cleveland in February of 1964. I vividly remember gathering with my family to watch the Beatles on the Ed Sullivan Show those three Sunday nights in February and immediately falling in love with them and their music. I even remember intuiting the connection between the Beatles and my only other music love before that – Chuck Berry. The driver of my nursery van used to' listen to rock and roll, and Chuck Berry had become my favorite!

My older sister, Marcia, immediately went out the day after the Ed Sullivan Show to buy *Meet the Beatles*. I used to sneak into her room when she wasn't there to listen to it without her permission. I used to take her badminton racquet (again, naturally, without her permission) to "play guitar" along with the Beatles.

Incidentally, Marcia had been offered a ticket to the Beatles concert in Cleveland in 1965 – except that the concert fell on Yom Kippur eve that year. My grandmother threatened to go into mourning ('sit shiva') for her if my parents let her go. Marcia finally saw Paul McCartney in concert in Washington, DC, during his 2002 tour. She had front row seats and is completely convinced that Paul looked directly at her and smiled at her...as if to make up for the lost glories of thirty-seven years ago!

Back in 1964, one Cleveland radio station featured a "Beatles countdown" every night at 9:00 p.m., during which they played Beatles songs according to some mail-in request formula. As an eight-year-old kid, this was past my bedtime, so I'd listen to it every night under the covers. They have been my music ever since.

The Beatles' music inspired me, many years later, to form my own rock and roll band, called Shake, Rabbis and Roll – or, as it is affectionately known among its aficionados and assorted roadies, SR2 (which is the logo featured on the bass drum).

SR2 got its humble start in the spring of 1991 when I received my first guitar as an anniversary present from my wife, Nellie. After a few months of lessons (the only training I was destined to receive), I had mastered – well, *learned* – four chords. I remember them to this day: G–Em–C–D. Upon being told by my teacher, a classical guitarist named Eve Weiss, that this was the basic chord pattern for many old rock songs, I was determined to form a band to play at an upcoming rock and roll party at the Pelham Jewish Center, the congregation where I then served as Rabbi. SR2's live repertoire contains no Jewish or religious music – just good, old-fashioned rock and roll!

The first lineup of SR2 consisted of me on rhythm guitar (with four chords under my belt, I could consider myself a "rhythm guitarist"); my old friend, Rabbi Larry Sebert, who had drummed in the pit band of many of the theatrical productions I directed during summers at Camp Ramah in Wisconsin; my teacher, Eve Weiss, on lead guitar; and a Jesuit-educated friend, Spencer Hayman, who was a wicked bass player. Shake, Rabbis and Roll was born.

We played four songs at our first gig, and raised money for a *tzedakah* (charity) project. In doing this, we established a pattern for all future performances: always provide a redemptive aspect for the gig, so that 'technically' people are not actually coming to hear *us* play, but rather are turning out on behalf of some worthwhile project.

We continue to perform to raise *tzedakah* (charity) for a variety of worthy causes. We have performed on behalf of a church soup kitchen on 111th & Broadway in New York; at the West End Café in Manhattan, where we raised nearly $2,000 for World Trade Center relief; and we've done quite a few shows to benefit Mazon (which means "food" in Hebrew), an organization which distributes food to needy people of all faiths.

While SR2 is primarily a cover band, performing rock and roll classics from the '50s, '60s and '70s (as well as more contemporary music), we've recently begun to perform songs that carry the songwriting credit, "Words and music by Robbie Harris." We recently recorded a CD entitled, "Tales of the Upper West Side." Like our live repertoire, it doesn't feature religious music – just straight, good, old-fashioned rock and roll! But fear not; none of us will be quitting our proverbial "day jobs" any time soon!

Rabbi Robbie Harris, Age 48
New York, New York

Pondering Strawberry Fields
And Wandering Central Park

March 24, 2000 (as edited from my handwritten journal)

I write now from the first block of West 72nd Street at 7 a.m., smelling the smells, taking it all in. Central Park is in the foreground. I know where I am and feel as though it is so natural. Left my car on 71st Street in a garage. Not many folks out right now and it reminds me, just a bit, of London. I wonder what Yoko is doing right now. Does she know that someone who finds her soulmate so attractive is walking by? Doubt it. I will be taking photos in Central Park.

Must be garbage day. There's refuse out at the curb. Police emergency vehicles are already heralding, with their sirens, the day of tragedies about to be discovered. The smells of breakfast and coffee fill the air I breathe in. I'm okay, though almost too anxious with anticipation to eat. I've decided no pictures of the Dakota, it feels disrespectful somehow. Walking by it now...my God...it is ominous. Chilling thought of what happened – very cold – as I pass the side entry corridor. "No one beyond this point" sign is posted now where the devil's best friend went to get John's autograph so long ago. Whew, weird...onto Central Park straight ahead. Perhaps a long shot of the Dakota is in order. No, I think not. Best to respect and be quiet in vigil.

WOW! Right there! It is absolutely across the street from the Dakota, this bright, morning-lit field. The tears moisten the eyes, but not profusely. I feel more peace and warmth here than anything but that is what he was, correction – *IS* – all about. The direct, the simple...peace and love...

Well, now I have seen it, photographed it and I did discreetly shoot the "Imagine" mosaic with the Dakota in the background. This New York City, it is quite harmless and folks let you do what you will. No, no – no kissing the mosaic! Silly stuff…I'm just not that kind of fan (ha, ha). Besides, that sort of thing would raise him to saint level. Not his style at all, I respect that. I wouldn't bloody well want it either. Is his spirit here? Oh, yes, like anywhere else. Anything unusual? No. Remarkably, my feelings are of calm and peace. I have that morning "feel good on vacation" type of feeling. I feel terribly normal, actually. Except for that ice-cold feeling from walking by the Dakota earlier – that's the only thing.

Quite nice, this Strawberry Fields. I likely won't write more until I'm at the hotel pre-festival. Coming into the city, **9**'s followed me. Full service fill-up at the New Jersey service center on the Turnpike. He stopped it at…you guessed it, $9. So I tipped him, not sure what else to do and he thanked me. It's so peaceful and tranquil here in the park. A small sparrow hopped near to see if I had food, then he fluttered away. I asked him – "John?" – and he hopped closer. Oh, well, one can only – as the mosaic says – "Imagine."

Now soaking up the natural art and beauty that is Central Park. Many runners out now. This is their time and the stairs of the park, mixed with the hills and trees, is giving my weary-from-driving-1,120-miles legs a good stretch. This is the peaceful; this is the calming, a great restorative time from the hassles of a corporate living and to settle before the emotions of the festival.

Meeting up with my friends around 4:30 p.m. before Beatlefest opens. I simply LOVE morning – new beginnings, a day to live and feel every minute of. At about 2:30 a.m., it dawned on me why I am here Friday and not on Sunday. Today is 3/24/00. Add it up…it equals *nine*. Yeah, you got it. And Sunday is too holy a day – not very John. He is more like a Friday – a fun, alive kind of day. That's him – see what I mean? Not anything big, or tea and biscuits with

Yoko…just little things meaningful to no one but me, and that's what is lovely and spiritual about it. It is funny to watch people too. New Yorkers are bustling, hustling, looking so busy and New York City-ish. Cell phones, dogs and all – very cute, very trendy, very Madison Avenue, as programmed. They seem such a state of very ordinary, predictable and typical, which is horribly amusing to me.

More I write here in New York City as I am waiting for FAO Schwarz to open to buy something for my seven-year-old son. Sitting, as it happens, on a rather chilly concrete bench in front of the Plaza Hotel. Hmmm, seems to me that some incredibly famous folks stayed here from time to time in the '60s…Get pictures of the outside, gorgeous hotel inside, though it would be too tacky to take photos inside, so I don't. Very lovely day in New York City. A nice breeze as well. A couple of my friends at home would so love all of this – writing, drinking coffee. I noted on 58th Street, discreetly located very near the Plaza Hotel, the business of a clairvoyant, a very small sign – low key. I've got to wonder if big money and/or famous people use that person for advice preceding the big deal?

Just enjoying sitting in the heart of it here, the sounds, sights and smells of the city: horse manure and diesel fuel. No opinion, just the dominating aromas and then there is no distinct odor – another day. I'm on my way to the cup of coffee recommended by the concierges of the Plaza. They told me, "That way," and I headed towards Sixth Avenue (Avenue of the Americas). Thought it would be right on 59th Street, the way they were talking, but not so. As I paused at the corner of 59th and Sixth, I thought, turn down here – there's a McDonald's sign, at least they'll have coffee. Then I get this cosmic intuition. That uncanny way, when I am open and receptive, that I have of habit, not necessarily because of John, mind you!

I make an instinctive judgment or decision to get the very thing, in this case a cup of coffee, from the Rock 'n Roll

Deli, which the concierges vaguely pointed me in the direction of. Now noting performers in yellow suits at Trump Towers opposite where I sit, readying for a show of some type, or having just done one, I imagine. The sounds of morning are roaring to life in this city of tough folks. They aren't that tough, though; it's just a front. They're like any other Americans. I can feel that.

Moved to a sunnier spot. Shadow of Trump Towers made cold where I was writing. This area is much unlike earlier through Central Park. Yet still as worthy to put to paper. Well, well, well…just spied a double-decker tour bus like those in London. Did they copy the Englanders? Possibly, I don't know. Still yet another hour before FAO Schwarz opens. Perhaps I'll sit on a bench in Central Park and meditate. This concrete bench is so hard on my ass and has no back on it.

Back in Central Park. Much more comfy, as comfy as one can be on a wooden bench. And now I see that this was likely the area that the trio of John, Paul and Ringo did wander and pose for cameras way back in 1964, before many New Yorkers would've taken serious note of them. Before their appearance on the Ed Sullivan Show, before the mania manifested itself across America. (Good! Smell of horse dung and diesel fuel not present in the park here.) Anyway, the bridge where *they* stood is in view and I see now how the Dakota would be in some of the photos. Just more fodder for good fictional writing. You can write well without going to places, but having gone now I can write more believably.

Did some artsy window-shopping in the Plaza: Cartiers, etc., and there was a print store on Sixth Avenue. Thankfully, nothing's open – but then I'm not buying here, only at FAO Schwarz for my boy. Suspect I will be getting out of New York City around lunchtime. Then back to New Jersey to find the hotel that will be my home for the next two days. No need to return here Sunday. I do want to note that street vendors are starting to set up their wares just outside

Central Park here. Perhaps I could look over the goods prior to stopping at the toy store. I'm just sitting here doing time, watching the wheels go 'round. The car wheels, vehicles of all kinds, did John from his windows in the Dakota see that as he looked out? Is that where the inspiration of the phrase lies? Perhaps. Who knows? Only John knows for sure.

I am so spiritually fulfilled and relaxed. This pilgrim's journey is complete. Am I now ready to party at Beatlefest? Not sure I will enjoy the marketplace but I feel I will be more tuned to the music than excitement over merchandise, but that is what the Beatles are all about – the music. Like I've said before – the rest is window dressing.

Mission accomplished in FAO Schwarz. Purchase of a fuzzy Gengar in hand. I now sit in Strawberry Fields, three and a half hours hence, where I was this morning at 7 a.m. All manner of folks are here. Now it is beautiful to see so many others loving him, yet I enjoyed my private time earlier. They gather in the circle, take photos. Some lay down flowers. The Dakota stands in the background, as ominous as ever. Crowds gather, it is good to see, but my visit is over and the virgin pilgrimage done. I feel ordained somehow – how strange I feel. Just a "me-within-myself" kind of thing. I wonder if Yoko ever looks out and sees all who still care? Wonder? Pay tribute? Most pause momentarily. Some take photos and are on their way. One woman appears to be the self-appointed caretaker of the site. She arranges flowers and people take photos. I notice windows open at the Dakota. Who else lives there? Famous and/or rich, they are the only ones who could afford it.

Time to go. The woman "caretaker" says she couldn't be happier. It is her hobby, she says. Occasionally, someone starts to sing *Strawberry Fields Forever*. So goes the world. Some cry, a few are mesmerized, most just look, then proceed. What must John think of all this? "Load of crap!" is what I hear from somewhere…John? Are you really here? "But very nice." Okay…that was different. How could I hear that? Whatever that just was – kudos to you, John! You didn't create a pocket of hate as you worried about in 1966. You left lorries full of love all over the world. Some larger than others, but so many, many pockets, and LOVE IS ALL you need. I must stop now. Don't want to start tearing up. The "caretaker" has finished her affectionate decorative art of flowers and photos with some lyrics. She is gone until tomorrow, I suspect. Now on to my first Beatle festival in the Meadowlands, NJ, to celebrate John's LIFE and the Beatles!

Sharon Richards, Age 37
Orlando, Florida

Sharon Richards holds a degree in Broadcasting but her heart is held by John Lennon. Sharon works full-time at the newest Hard Rock Cafe attraction in Orlando – The Vault. She "hangs out" with lots of cool Beatles memorabilia and is one of two Beatle experts on staff. She is also an award-winning poet, Poetry Editor for *Rooftop Sessions* and author of two poetry/short story books about John Lennon.

Check out her web site at: www.dropforgedlennon.com.

Does It Matter How?

In this state
Of my brain
You seem to come alive
Each still I turn
To see you
Framed in time
Smiling back at me
Saying

"Live it
Love it my luv
Dance in the passion
The music makes you
Whole and free
Join with me
Your form is not required
Nothing for the journey
But
Imagination!"

Sharon Richards, Age 40
Orlando, Florida

Just A Place

Sitting in the imagine spot
So much I have of you
Full circle I come to meet myself
Love
The light shines on
Just gimme the truth
Strawberry Fields Central Park
Just a place
One and everyone we feel your embrace
Taking the moment to hesitate
In timelessness we find
Together
No boundaries exist
My soul wrapped in pure love
Through days warm, sweet
Cold and brisk

Sharon Richards, Age 40
Orlando, Florida

(This article originally appeared in the December 1998 issue of Delta Air Lines' Sky magazine.)

Mickey's Magical Mystery Tour

Tough journalist–or ogling fan?
Managing editor–or hard-core Beatlemaniac?

When my parents drag out the old home movies, they always laugh to see 4-year-old me playing a toy guitar and singing "I Want to Hold Your Hand." It used to embarrass me, but now I see it as a pivotal moment. You see, it was shot just a few weeks after John Lennon, Paul McCartney, George Harrison and Ringo Starr—The Beatles—performed that very song for the first time on American television. Under the influence of my then-teenage brother Don, I tuned in—like millions of other Americans—to "The Ed Sullivan Show" on Sunday evening, February 9, 1964, and I "got that something. I think you'll understand."

As I got older, my fascination with The Beatles grew (despite a short, meaningless fling with The Monkees). Don moved on to The Rolling Stones and R&B, but I didn't waver. I inherited his Beatle albums and then began buying my own. I agonized over their breakup in 1970 and then followed Paul's solo career as I longed for a reunion. While at college, I began to understand and appreciate John a bit more, only to see him tragically taken away from us. In 1990, I saw a Beatle (Paul) live in concert for the first time. More recently, Beatle fans like me were rewarded for our patience with the long-awaited *Beatles Anthology*, even if it was only a reunion of the pseudo kind.

The *Anthology* was satisfying, but it made me realize that one major item was missing from my Beatle résumé: a pilgrimage to the Land of Fab, England. Then an e-mail message came my way, advertising a trip to London and

Liverpool to follow in The Beatles' footsteps. Needless to say, I signed up right away, but I wondered: Do I go as a journalist or as a fan?

Or could I be both?

Day 1: Henley-on-Thames

After flying all night, we arrive at London's Heathrow Airport, collect our luggage and board our coach for the beginning of our tour. There will be no time for catching up on sleep. My body clock is confused—it's been a hard night's day.

Mingling with the tour group, I try to balance being sociable with maintaining a detached, journalistic exterior. Two of my tourmates, Steve and Maria, sense my apprehension and try to break the ice. But still I'm reluctant. Who *are* these people? Hey, I'm a Beatle fan, but these people seem, well, fanatical—to the extreme, in some cases.

Our first tour stop is Henley-on-Thames, a quaint village west of London that George calls home. We make our way to his Friar Park estate. To our dismay, George apparently isn't going to invite us in for tea and scones, so we mill about outside the front gate. Steve decides to peer into George's mailbox. "Hey, George has mail!" he yells, as I roll my eyes. "It's a letter from Hawaii." Steve proceeds to record this discovery with his video camera—I don't know whether this violates any British postal laws.

Day 2: London

Today, I meet more people on the tour. They're from all walks of life, ages 15 to 50. Many have made this trip before, several of them *many* times before. They're all here because a band touched them and their lives—a band that has not performed as a unit for nearly 30 years. Can you imagine anyone touring Great Britain in the year 2028 to see where Ginger, Sporty, Scary and the rest of the Spice rack lived and shopped for their first platform shoes? I can't, but I know Beatle tours will still be going strong.

This afternoon, we hop on the coach for a tour of The Beatles' London, hosted by the president of the London Beatles Fan Club, an enthusiastic chap named Richard, proud holder of the title "Beatles Brain of Britain." Even the mundane Beatle sites get a rise out of him.

Like, for instance, a tree. But not just any tree. It's a tree in the 18th-century gardens of Chiswick House, where The Beatles shot promo films (the forerunner of music videos) for the songs "Rain" and "Paperback Writer" in 1966. Everyone takes advantage of this photo op, posing with the tree and with our tourmate Mark. Why Mark? Well, I guess if you can't have your photo taken with John Lennon, then why not with someone who tries to look like him? *Bizarro Beatle.*

The next major stop is Marylebone Station, where the train-station scenes from *A Hard Day's Night* were filmed. The opening sequence of the lads running along a street, chased by screaming fans, was also shot here. To the confusion of several passersby, four guys from our tour, along with several screaming gals, oblige us by re-creating this bit of cinematic history, complete with "George"— rather, Vinny—falling.

A trip to The Beatles' London would not be complete without a stop at EMI's Abbey Road Studios. For now, we have to be content with looking at the exterior, adding graffiti to the wall and having our photographs taken as we quickly stroll across the famous zebra crossing. Quickly because Abbey Road is a busy street, and London motorists can get a bit impatient with all the posing.

We leave Abbey Road, but just for a little while. After a few more stops—including 34 Montagu Square, where Ringo, John, Yoko and even Jimi Hendrix lived (but not all at the same time)—we pull up to 3 Abbey Road again. But this time we are ushered in and led back to Studio 2, where The Beatles recorded most of their songs, from "Love Me Do" to "The End." Abbey Road isn't open to the general public, but our tour leaders get around that little bit of a roadblock by booking us as recording artists. Yes, recording artists. The EMI people, of course, are on to us, but thanks to a light schedule and our persuasive tour leaders, they let the charade go on.

The recording session, however, isn't a complete charade. While we were on the coach this afternoon, Sgt. Pepper's Band, a Beatle cover band from Brazil, was in Studio 2 to lay down the basic backing tracks for "Hey Jude." (Yeah, purists, I know the original wasn't recorded at Abbey Road—but so what?) After we arrive, the band's "Paul" overdubs the lead vocal while we add the "*nah, nah, nah, nah-nah-nah-nah, nah-nah-nah-nah, hey Jude*" and handclaps at the end. We get it right after only three takes. Now we can all say we've recorded at Abbey Road. ("Hey, that's me, right there on the fade-out! Can't you hear me?")

Day 3: London

Time for a walking tour of central London Beatle sites with Richard (who does this for a living), and the beginning of what many of us rather sarcastically call our "Tour of Doors." This tour has nothing to do with Jim Morrison but everything to do with lack of access. With rare exceptions, our tours leave us standing outside various structures only to gawk, hear a spiel and take a photo—of a door. Today, we see the doors of MPL Communications (Paul's offices), what was formerly Trident Studios (where "Hey Jude" was actually recorded) and the former Apple Corps Ltd. building (site of the rooftop concert from *Let It Be*).

Although we never see a Beatle in the flesh during our stay, we do see the offspring of a Beatle. Our tour leader, Charles, scores us tickets to "The Jack Docherty Show," a kind of low-budget British version of America's "Late Night With David Letterman." This evening's show features none other than John's son Julian, who performs with his band.

The evening, our last in London, is topped off by a concert featuring a series of Beatle cover bands from around the world—some who just try to sound like The Beatles and others who try to look like them, too. *Yawn*. I bow out early.

Day 4: Liverpool

We arrive in Liverpool by mid-afternoon and make our way to 20 Forthlin Road, Paul's boyhood home. At last, we move past a door! This 1950s terrace house, which was opened to the public in July as a National Trust property, is now occupied by its caretaker, John Halliday, a Beatle fan who beat out many others for this privileged job. "Sit anywhere you like," he tells us cordially. "You can even sit on the bed in Paul's room. Of course, it's not really *his* bed."

At this point, several of my tourmates get emotional.

None of the furnishings here belonged to the McCartneys, but all are faithful to the proper time period, including the television and record player in the front parlor—where, we discover, Paul and John wrote "Love Me Do" and "I Saw Her Standing There."

After our 40 minutes are up, we drag Maria out of Paul's bedroom (it takes three of us) and head to the grand Britannia Adelphi Hotel—well, grand for Liverpool. This week, it is the nerve center for International Beatle Week and the Mersey Beatle Convention, which attract thousands of Beatle fanatics from around the world every year at the end of August.

This evening, we head over to the Liverpool Institute for Performing Arts, formerly the Liverpool Institute, which was a high school for boys that counted Paul and George among its alumni. After years of decay, the school was rescued, thanks in part to Paul, and is now known as Paul's "Fame" school. The reason for our visit: another concert of Beatle cover bands in the well-appointed Paul McCartney Auditorium.

Day 5: Liverpool

This morning, we were to have our own "Magical Mystery Tour" of Liverpool Beatle sites, riding on a coach that is an exact replica of the one The Beatles used in the film *Magical Mystery Tour*. As I said, we *were* to have a Magical Mystery Tour, but our coach has broken down—one of the problems with using 30-year-old vehicles. Our guide, a charming lady named Hilary, gives us her best effort with an abbreviated walking tour in the morning and a quick hit-and-miss tour on a hired coach in the afternoon.

At first, I am miffed, but as it turns out, the problems we experience have an interesting effect on me and my tourmates—bringing us closer together. My journalistic indifference is definitely melting away, and the fan in me is starting to come out as I get to know the others.

Today's harried tour includes places we'll remember: the former Oxford Street Maternity Hospital, where John was born; "Mendips," where John lived with his Aunt Mimi from 1946 to 1963; the former Liverpool College of Art, where John went to school and where he met Cynthia Powell, his first wife; Ye Cracke, the pub where John drank his way through art school and courted Cyn; and the former Mount Pleasant Registry Office, where John married Cyn. I guess the service station where he put air in his bike tires has been torn down. Otherwise, I'm sure we would've seen it.

Other highlights: St. Peter's Church and Church Hall, where John was introduced to Paul on July 6, 1957, after a church fête featuring John's band, the Quarry Men; "the shelter in the middle of a roundabout" at Penny Lane; and a continuation of our Tour of Doors, including Ringo's and George's birthplaces and other Beatle childhood residences.

Day 6: Liverpool

I decide to skip a daylong auction of Beatle memorabilia (I can't afford it anyway) so that I can spend time on Mathew Street, the "Birthplace of The Beatles." Here, I step down into the deep, dark reaches of the reconstructed Cavern Club (the original was demolished in 1973), where The Beatles performed nearly 300 times between 1961 and '63, and where Brian Epstein, who later became their manager, first saw them perform. It is roughly on the same site as the original and, based on the photos I've seen, looks pretty authentic.

The spirit of Mathew Street, however, is dampened a bit by those trying to cash in on spurious Beatle connections. Near the revered Cavern are places such as Lennon's Bar, the Abbey Road pub and the Rubber Soul Oyster Bar (of course, it's well-documented that The Beatles were under the influence of shellfish when they recorded *Rubber Soul*), none of which have anything to do with The Beatles' era. I stay away from these places, but like a true local, or "Scouser," I do drop in at The Grapes for a pint, just as The Beatles did between Cavern sets—the club having been alcohol-free and The Grapes the nearest pub. *Cheers*!

This evening, we venture out to hear, *sigh*, more cover bands. You see, I'm a fan of the real thing, and hearing all these guys trying to do their best John, Paul, George and Ringo is not why I'm here. But tonight is different: A band from Sweden, Lenny Pane, turns me around with their ingenuity and showmanship. Plus, they're doing Beatle songs you rarely, if ever, hear played live—songs from the post-1966 "Studio Years"—and they're doing them exceptionally well, considering their complexities. Heck, I halfway expect them to launch into the cryptic "Revolution 9" from the "White Album," but that would be too much.

Day 7: Liverpool

Today, we have a special treat: a garden fête on the grounds of the Strawberry Field Children's Home, a place where John played as a child and that he would later immortalize in song. The weather couldn't be better, and we all enjoy playing carnival games, eating strawberries and cream, listening to bands, and having "nothing to get hung about."

In the evening, we go to see a performer we've been hearing about since we arrived: Gary Gibson, a John Lennon impersonator. Walking to the venue, all I can conjure up is that this will be the equivalent of "hunka, hunka burnin' love" in a sequined jumpsuit on a Vegas stage. I'm wrong again. This guy looks like, sounds like, acts like and (if I could get close enough) probably even smells like John. Unlike many of the other faux Beatles I've seen, he ad-libs, which adds a lot to his performance. It's spooky.

Day 8: Liverpool

This morning, I grab a taxi to Albert Dock to see The Beatles Story—a multimedia exhibition that takes you from boyhood to breakup and beyond. It's like walking through a Beatle time line, but with a gift shop.

The afternoon is filled with the Mersey Beatle Convention at the Adelphi, a feast for Beatle memorabilia collectors, which can be dangerous if you get carried away. One tourmate spends all her cash, overdraws her checking account and maxes out her credit cards. (Baby, *you'll need* a rich man.)

In addition to dealers selling everything from Beatle boots to Beatle bootleg (rather, "import") CDs, the convention features more cover bands, of course, and a series of guest speakers, including Bob Wooler, the former Cavern DJ; Allan Williams, The Beatles' first manager, who makes a living billing himself as "The Man Who Gave The Beatles Away" and charging people like me a pound for his autograph; Alistair Taylor, who was Brian Epstein's right-hand man and later helped run Apple; Alf Bicknell, The Beatles' chauffeur from the mid-'60s, who also hung out with our group in London; Julia Baird, John's half-sister, who does bear a striking resemblance to her famous sibling; and Alan Parsons, a recording engineer for The Beatles during their *Let It Be–Abbey Road* sessions who went on to work on Pink Floyd's *Dark Side of the Moon* and his own Alan Parsons Project.

Following the convention, we are treated to a show by The Merseybeats, an *actual* Liverpool band from the '60s, complete with the group's two original frontmen.

Day 9: Liverpool

Since this is our last full day in the Land of Fab, my tourmates and I try to take care of last-minute must-sees and must-do's. Evan, a rising freshman in college who's here with his mother, Linda, and younger sister Alyssa, heads back to Penny Lane for a haircut. Linda records the moment on film and promises to send the barber a photo. After all, he'll need it to show everyone this "head he's had the pleasure to know."

As for me, I decide that I must take the ferry that travels across the River Mersey, connecting Liverpool and Wirral and made famous by Beatle contemporaries Gerry and the Pacemakers with their song "Ferry 'Cross the Mersey." So I head toward the docks in the drizzling rain—the first such weather we've experienced.

I pay for my round-trip fare, get on board and immediately go up top so I'll have a better view of the Royal Liver (pronounced "LYE-ver") Building, adorned with its mythical Liver Birds. By then, the rain has stopped, but it is still gray, which actually adds a bit to the experience.

Back on dry land, I set out to locate the building that once housed NEMS, the Epstein family record shop that Brian managed. I find something that looks like the right place, but I'm not sure. So I wander in to what turns out to be a lingerie/adult boutique. The clerk is very helpful and verifies the site as he goes about nonchalantly marking prices on various, er, sexual playthingies.

I make it back to the hotel just in time for a Q&A session with Neil Innes and John Halsey—better known as Ron Nasty and Barry Wom of The Rutles, a parody of The Beatles' music and life created by Innes and Monty Python's Eric Idle back in the mid-'70s. Later in the afternoon, "Ron" and "Barry" join The Bootleg Rutles *(a cover band of a parody band?)* onstage at The Cavern.

After a quick dinner, several of my new-found friends and I head back to The Cavern one last time. After a while, the heat and dankness of the club start to get to us, so we head up to the street for some air. As I shoot the breeze with Skip and Greg, four "apparitions" emerge from the darkness at the head of Mathew Street. As they move toward The Cavern, we can make out only a familiar outline of each. Can it be? Have we somehow traveled back to 1963? We rub our eyes. They look just like John, Paul, George and Ringo carrying instruments on their backs, heading to a show. "John" is even wearing his trademark cap. Suddenly, reality hits. It's 1998, and the foursome is The Beats, a cover band from Argentina who really look the part (especially to our friend Carolyn, who doesn't want to escape this time warp).

For a moment, though, I feel I really know what it was like back then. I have to choose, I realize, and I do: I'm a fan. Despite all the tourist traps along Mathew Street, despite my journalist's ingrained cynicism, despite more than 30 years having passed, it suddenly connects. It all comes together, the '60s and the '90s, my singing "I Want to Hold Your Hand" as a 4-year-old and my being at The Cavern at 38. I have known *about* The Beatles for most of my life, but now that I've seen their London and Liverpool, I feel like I *know* them.

Mickey McLean, Age 38
Greensboro, North Carolina
September, 1998

Mickey McLean is the managing editor of Delta Air Lines' Sky *magazine. He lives in Greensboro, North Carolina, with a wife who tolerates The Beatles and a young daughter who adores their music.*

Defining Moments

My mother is a Beatles nut, a tested and certified Beatlemaniac. She'll blush when she reads this, say "Megan…" in that fake disparaging tone, all while trying to contain her grin.

Accept it, Mom, embrace it; after all, you raised a daughter just like you.

I first became aware of the mania when I was about ten. Paul McCartney was coming to town, and tickets were nearly impossible to get. Mom heard on the radio that a jewelry store one hundred miles away was going to be selling tickets to those willing to camp in their parking lot overnight. Within minutes Mom had thrown blankets, pillows, three kids and a husband into the minivan and was on the highway. She got the tickets, but my brothers and I began to question her sanity, especially after we discovered that she wasn't planning on taking us with her to the concert.

The next few years were relatively calm. Mom and I went to Beatles cover band concerts and watched the *Anthology* videos many times over. Christmas and birthday gifts were never a problem; if the gift was Beatles related, the odds were that Mom would love it.

Insanity re-emerged when I was seventeen. The catalyst was a brochure that arrived in the mail, advertising a ten-day Beatles tour from London to Liverpool, coinciding with International Beatles Week. After reading the brochure, Mom fell backwards onto the bed, moaning about how much she wanted, and how little she could afford, to go. I, however, started calculating — I'll jump at any chance to travel.

"If you use your savings and I work all summer, we can pay for the tour."

"What about extras like food and cabs — oh, those cute little British taxicabs…"

"Well, we could sell everything in the attic at a yard sale."

So that's exactly what we did. Off went the seldom-used ping-pong table, the childhood toys and discarded furniture. The rest of the family supported the idea, believing that the trip would cleanse the mania from our systems. In August, the two of us flew off to England.

For ten days, Mom was a teenager once more. She had her picture taken with Beatles cover bands from around the world, stayed up late dancing in nightclubs and drank pints with her daughter, our age difference disappearing with every sip. The tour was thorough; we saw *their* houses and *their* schools, and even recorded with a Beatles cover band in Abbey Road Studios. Mom had finally made her pilgrimage, and she had never been happier. We returned to the States drained to exhaustion, already planning to return the next year.

The family was dumbfounded: "What do you mean you want to go again?" But Mom and I refused to listen. Egged on by a mother-daughter team in Boston whom we had met on the previous tour, we booked our flight yet again. One last fling before I started college.

We've traveled separately since then; I to various countries, Mom always returning to her beloved Britain with my father in tow. We have no regrets of the time we spent in England, or of the hoops we had to jump through in order to get there. Our relationship changed during those traveling days. I discovered the teenager inside the mother, an equal, and that is what she has remained — a travel partner, a friend, and a devoted Beatlemaniac.

Recently, Paul came to town again, and this time, Mom took me along.

Meg Hensley, Age 23
Raleigh, North Carolina

Staring At The Gates Of Strawberry Fields

The faint strains of *I Want to Hold Your Hand* came drifting into the dining room from the radio in my older brother's room. I called out to him and asked who was singing. He said it was a new group from England called the Beatles. I stood up, walked out of the dining room and into my brother's room, and simply stood there listening.

I grew up in a small town in North Carolina. I never saw the Beatles perform together, but the fact that they existed in the world completely altered my life. I started falling asleep listening to my transistor radio. I sat on the floor in front of the TV, waiting impatiently for the Ed Sullivan Show to begin, and when I caught my first glimpse of John Lennon I chose him for "my Beatle," and he remains so to this day. I threw my books down each afternoon after school while simultaneously turning on my record player to listen to the Beatles.

They controlled my life. Although most of my friends liked the Beatles, only two others were as obsessed as I was. We searched the newspaper for articles on the Beatles, bought Beatle fan magazines so we could cut out the photos and paste them into scrapbooks and create our own captions for them. We anxiously awaited the release of each new 45, and we walked to Roses department store to buy our copies as soon as they were stocked. We began writing plays about them, with each of us trying to give "our Beatle" the best and wittiest dialogue. If we weren't together, we called each other on the phone to read the latest scene we had written.

We bought the four Beatle dolls and carried them around with us and placed them atop our desks at school. For my birthday I begged my parents for a portable tape player so I could make tapes of my records. I carried my tape player everywhere, even across the country to Oregon on a family car trip. My parents listened tolerantly to the Beatles for 6,000 miles.

My friends and I took turns having slumber parties, and the three of us who were Beatles-obsessed would choose someone to be Ringo and we would perform for the other girls, using our tennis racquets as guitars. Bitter arguments arose because the others had to watch the performances as the audience, or just stand at the side as Brian Epstein. We entered the talent show as the Beatles at our elementary school. We began buying packs of bubble gum cards and memorizing the Beatle facts written on the back, quizzing each other to make sure we had mastered every bit of information. I persuaded my best friend to hide in the movie theater with me so we could watch *A Hard Day's Night* three times consecutively.

Even during those early years, I instinctively knew the Beatles were superior to other groups. I could not express it at that age, but I knew they were talented and "artsy." As a few years passed and as the Beatles changed their appearance, we did, too. We began wearing mini-skirts and boots and wearing our hair long. We believed that our "real lives" would begin as soon as we got older and could get to London. I contemplated every remark John Lennon made, and I was entranced with his irreverent attitude and opinions. I continued to buy every record the Beatles released, and even now, a particular song will bring back memories of a certain book I was reading at that time, or how I was feeling at that stage in my life.

Although the Beatles were an integral part of my life during high school and college, I never made it to England until I traveled with my daughter Megan in 1998 on the Magical Mystery Tour. She had been inundated with the Beatles' music throughout her childhood, and now, to my delight, she wanted to see the places described in their songs. The entire trip to London and Liverpool was incredible, not just seeing those places I had heard about all those years, but also spending eleven days with other Beatle fanatics!

The single most moving and poignant experience for me was when I glanced out of our bus window and found myself staring at the red gates of Strawberry Fields. I sensed that many of the people in our group felt the same way, because no one had warned us that we were going to park in front of the gates; we were simply driving along a quiet, tree-lined road in Liverpool, and when I looked back at the other people on the bus, I knew they had the same reaction.

The Beatles are still very important to me, and my friends and I incessantly discuss their music and personal lives. Even though we went on the Magical Mystery Tour again in 1999, we plan more trips to England; after all, we have not yet seen the interior of John Lennon's childhood home on Menlove Avenue.

But nothing can or will ever replace the enchantment of those first few years after the Beatles arrived in America. We go to concerts now, and travel to Liverpool, but simply turning on the radio and hearing one of their earliest songs brings the extreme exhilaration and joy of 1964 crashing back to me. I feel that the Beatles, through the airwaves, sent messages to those in my generation, but only some of us "got it." I sometimes idly speculate about what it would have been like if there had been no Beatles, but it is unimaginable. John, Paul, George, and Ringo came, it was meant to be, and they were *ours*. In my life I've loved them all.

Carolyn Hensley, Age 50
Raleigh, North Carolina

A Liverpool Tale

When I was a young lad, my babysitter was George Harrison's mother. We lived next door to George and his family in Upton Green, Speke, Liverpool. Mrs. Harrison would look after me quite a bit and was my babysitter for several years, as my mother was not a well person.

Mrs. Harrison was very interested in opera and would play opera for me to try to get me to sleep. I knew George very well. I was there when George got his very first car, a blue Ford Anglia. This was before the family moved to Mackets Lane in Hale Wood, Liverpool.

We still have a postcard that George sent to my mother while he was in America.

Robert Gregory, Age 54
Liverpool, England

And I Remember

And I remember…

Dad has always been a great fan. He was lucky to be born in 1957. He has great memories, such as seeing Beatles movies in the theatre, the people going crazy when the Beatles came near his home to give a concert, buying each new album, and he and his friends listening to the Beatles on the radio every day.

Anyway, I didn't have the same luck! I was born January 30, 1990. I am now 13 years old. As I said above, my dad is a great fan. He was listening to their songs on the stereo for as long as I can remember.

I was in fifth grade. My dad came to me with an audio system just for me, a Discman…what we all dream about in fifth grade. One day, while my dad was working, I took the *White Album* from his collection, and I listened to *Back in the USSR*. Minutes later I had listened to the complete album.

I remember…

The next day, nothing much happened except I did tell my dad that I listened to the *White Album* and it was incredible. Days later, the Beatles' "**1**" CD was out in stores. My dad came home with it. A friend at work gave it to him as a gift. I was listening to it all day – that's when the Beatlemania started flowing through my veins! I felt just like the teens did in 1964, when the Beatles took America – and the world – by storm.

Months ago I took some guitar classes. I didn't even have a guitar. When I saw the *Anthology* DVD, I forgot about everything else and started practicing myself.

Since we all can remember...

Being any age and loving the Beatles. The Beatles are described to us just as they really are: a great band, the greatest band of all time, Lennon-McCartney, Beatlemania, their wonderful movies, the many albums they recorded. We all have heard about the genius of John Lennon, the deepness of Paul McCartney, the elegance of George Harrison, and the kindness of Ringo Starr. We all can remember even one day in our lives when we have heard a Beatles song or two, and the songs made us happy for even an hour or two.

I somehow know that I was not really born in 1990. I was actually born in 1964. I'm sure of it.

The magic of the Beatles is timeless and ageless, and with every minute that goes by, the Beatlemania in me grows stronger than ever...

Alicia Navarro, Age 13
Mexico

Reliving The Magic

"Sit back, you are now being transported back to 1964, the year the Beatles came to America…"

As these words left my mouth, I glanced at my teacher. I began to present my sixth-grade final project: *The History of the Fab Four.* I suppose it was an unusual topic for a twelve-year-old to choose. Most of the kids opted to do their presentations on subjects like skateboarding or baseball cards. My mom taught me well. I chose the Beatles.

I kept my eyes on my teacher throughout the presentation. She was smiling. She had this look of nostalgia on her face. I'll never forget it. I knew that her mind was somewhere else far away, another time, another place. I couldn't believe that I was only twelve years old and I was stirring up such emotions in a 45-year-old woman. I later understood that it wasn't me stirring up these emotions in her. It was the Beatles.

I remember that while I was working on my project, my mom told me stories of how loud the screaming was that night at Shea Stadium. My teacher even sat me down after class to tell me how she felt when she watched them on the Ed Sullivan Show for the first time. I was amazed at the memories that the Beatles evoked in people who were around in the '60s and able to experience all this first-hand. When I looked at pictures of their Shea Stadium concert, and played sound clips from the Hollywood Bowl, I wished that I could have been there to experience it myself.

Even at twelve years old, I already understood the Beatles' enormous impact on people. Almost everyone from that time has their own unique connection to the band or their music. I was intrigued by all these stories – I believe that they instilled a love for the Beatles in me. They were, however, other people's stories. You could say I was a "second-hand" Beatles fan, and I wondered if, more than twenty years after their breakup, I could find my own connection to the Beatles.

I did.

Evan Schultz, Age 24
Currently residing in Izmir, Turkey

This is a photo of the actual PA license plate I got for my van when we lived in Philadelphia in the early '90s. It was cool when strangers would give us the thumbs-up!

Linda Schultz

Just One Look

I've been a Beatles fan since the summer of 1975, when I was nearly fourteen. (Perfect timing – talk about an influx of raging hormones!) I was aware of them as a child, certainly, and I do remember watching the Saturday morning cartoons, and *Yellow Submarine* when it came out in the theatres, but I was a bit young. The summer before my fourteenth birthday, I went to summer camp on Long Island and there was an older girl who was into the Beatles. She played their music for me and that sparked my interest.

It was John Lennon's voice that got me first – as a friend of mine has said, it sent chills directly to places unmentionable! And when I finally saw *A Hard Day's Night* around the time of my fourteenth birthday, that was *it*. I had only ever seen still pictures of John before and hadn't really heard him speak, just sing. But when I saw that movie, and saw him moving and talking and laughing – it was like tunnel vision. I didn't see *anything* or *anyone* else. I was smitten, totally and completely and utterly.

I liken it to the way a baby duck imprints on its mother – forever after, I have judged what I find sexy and attractive in men based on what I find sexy and attractive about John. Certainly the "packaging" was beautiful. I think John was extremely handsome and extremely sexy...and of course his stage stance – my God, that didn't hurt, did it?? But there were other things, too – his intelligence, his wit, his charm. I have always found intelligence to be extremely sexy – and the only man I ever met who lived up to the ideal I had set for myself (e.g., John – and that's a hell of an ideal for any other man to live up to, believe me!) was the man I eventually married, who is not only handsome and sexy, but very intelligent, too.

Another thing is that I owe John a lot in terms of what he gave me without ever knowing he did. Watching him made me realize that I didn't have to be apologetic about who *I* was, that it was okay to be me, and to be sassy and opinionated and passionate about the things I believed in. I think, strangely enough, that I saw a lot of things in him that I was unsure about in myself – and seeing how he handled those things made me more secure about my ability to handle similar things.

I know that John Lennon wasn't perfect – but he was beautiful, sexy, smart and honest, and those are all qualities I value very highly. My love for him is as real as any other love I have ever had, and it has never wavered, never varied, never changed since I was fourteen years old. I will love him and miss him for the rest of my life.

A small addendum to the above story: My mother has never quite understood my fascination with John. She knows I love the Beatles, but I sometimes get the impression that my particular infatuation for "the weird one," as she once put it many years ago, has completely baffled her. But very recently, something happened that made me believe that she might just "get it" after all...

At the Chicago Fest for Beatles Fans this year (2003), I finally made a very special purchase of an Astrid Kirschherr photograph I'd had my eye on for five years. For those of you familiar with Astrid's photos, it's the one of John standing in her attic, circa 1962, dressed in a black leather jacket, black turtleneck, black jeans and black boots, half in shadow. A truly beautiful photograph of a truly beautiful young man – at least I think so. At any rate, I had the photo professionally framed, and when it was done I took it to my parents' house to show off my purchase. I removed the picture from the bag I had carried it in and put it in my mother's hands...whereupon she gave a sharp gasp, and then turned to me, saying, "Oh...Susan...now I know what you see in him..."

I can't begin to tell you how very much that meant to me...it might have taken 28 years, but hearing that from my mother was probably one of the very best things she ever could have said to me. Thanks, Mom...I'm glad you *finally* understand.

Susan Ryan, Age 42
New York, New York

Susan Ryan is the Publisher and Editor-in-Chief of "Rooftop Sessions," a successful Beatles fan fiction webzine. She is a published writer and experienced editor of fiction, features, book and music reviews, editorials, and news articles. She has been a Beatleologist since 1975, has been the moderator of discussion panels on fan fiction at the New York, Chicago and Boston Fests for Beatles Fans, and was profiled in the Nov./Dec. 2001 issue of *Beatlefan Magazine* about this new phenomenon in publishing. She lives in New York City with her husband Jim and son Jamie.

Check out Rooftop Sessions at:

http://www.rooftopsessions.com/

I Want To Be A Paperback Writer

Here is my story as a Beatle fan…or, shall I say, as a *Beatlefreak*, as I am known among many of my friends. On this day, January 6, 2001, I am only twenty years old, but I feel so much older.

My story begins 1994, when I was thirteen years old. I don't think I listened to much music then. Kurt Cobain had died and Nirvana and Pearl Jam were basically the only bands I listened to in 1992. One day in 1994 I heard a song that I liked very much on the classic rock radio station. I liked it so much that I decided I had to find it in my parents' blanket chest where they kept all their old LPs. The album I grabbed was the Beatles. I knew the song had to be a Beatles song.

The first record I put on my little Fisher-Price record player (which still works to this day) was *Meet the Beatles*. The fast tempo and lively beat of *I Saw Her Standing There* really got me interested in the album. I could not find that song I had heard on the radio, though.

I returned to that blanket chest and found another Beatle album to play. And another. I spent the summer of 1994 listening to all of their LPs in search of that one song, but still I could not find it. Soon I forgot about the song and became a Beatles fan.

Quite an amazing way to discover the group, huh?

When my fourteenth birthday came around in September 1994, I got my first Beatle album: *Abbey Road* on CD. I remember telling my mother at the time that I didn't like that album, but I thanked her for it. I still cannot believe to this day that I said that because *Abbey Road* is one of my personal favorites now.

I remember spending my eighth grade year listening to the Beatles all the time. This is how I earned my nickname of *Beatlefreak*. I could answer every Beatles question friends would ask me. I was a walking Beatles encyclopedia. I had my own Beatle group, four girls who liked the band, but of course, I was the biggest fan. We each nicknamed ourselves after our favorite Beatle. Jennifer wanted to be John, but I had already claimed John, so she got Paul. Kim was George and Melissa was Ringo.

As we all entered high school the following year, Jennifer and I remained friends. We shared something else in common: we both had a crush on Sean Lennon *(sigh)*. We fought over who would get the beautiful picture of John in front of Lady Liberty that we spotted at the mall. I got it because I had saved my money.

Another memory of my early *Beatlefreak* years was that it took me two years to get all of their albums on CD. I worked really hard to get them, saving my allowance and all. Even my mother helped me – we had made a deal that if I attended a certain number of morning dance classes during my break in eighth grade, she would buy me the *Please Please Me* album. I did. She did.

I believe that I was destined to be a Beatles fan. I started down the path to becoming a Beatles fan at an early age. So I naturally believed that I had been a Beatles fan all my life; I just had to make the discovery myself.

I remember hearing *Revolution* and *Give Peace a Chance* in my mother's car when I was five years old. Believe it or not, I had my Barbies dancing to *Revolution!*

I also remember asking my mother, early in my Beatle craziness, which Beatle was dead. This was long before I heard about the "Paul is Dead" rumor. When she told me it was John, I cried because he is my favorite. Then she told me the story of where she was that evening. I was only three months old when John left. My mother played his *Double Fantasy* album many times. I do believe that playing music for your young children does have an effect on them. *Double Fantasy* has a special meaning for me.

Why do I like the Beatles so much? I don't think I would have been able to answer that when I was fourteen or fifteen. But my answer, as a twenty-year-old, is that they were a group ahead of their time. Every time I listen to their music, it always sounds fresh and new. It amazes me how four young men could create such great music that would shape the lives of millions of people. Perhaps not even that, but made people happy, as they did for me.

Any time I was angry or depressed, I always had these four men who cheered me up. To this day, whenever I hear one of their voices, my face lights up and I have a huge smile on my face. I credit them for helping me get through the tough years of adolescence, just as they had done for my mother and her friends.

I believe I have a purpose as a Beatle fan: to enjoy their music and to enjoy life. Because I am such a fan, it has brought my mother and me closer, something I love dearly. My mother often tells me, "I'm just sorry you didn't get to live through it all." I am, too, but I have the many stories she has told me and I never get tired of hearing them. I also have my own memories of experiencing *A Hard Day's Night* in the movie theatre – three times! The feeling I had when I saw John on the big screen is indescribable. It's so much fun to watch them on the big screen.

Another purpose I have as a Beatles fan is converting my friends – or at least making them aware of the impact the Beatles had on the world. I know my friends are sick of my ravings, but at least they listen.

I thank my mother for brainwashing her children, since we're all music fans in our own right. She laughs to this day about it.

Incidentally, I finally discovered in the summer of 2000 that the song I had been searching for back in 1994 was the Monkees' *Daydream Believer*.

Katie L. Myers, Age 20
Orlando, Florida
January 6, 2001

A Hard Day's Night

Marylebone Station,
running from limousines,
smothered with swarming girls
buzzing on footpaths.
shouting and cheering,
waving hands, some fainting.

Razor wit dialogue.
Conversations on a rattling train
On tracks folding out to open fields.

Flashes of freedom
explode into bubbles
tickling eyes with the Fab Four.

Hotel doors blocked.
Transistor radios blare.
Sobbing fans,
teenage girls, businessmen, old ladies,
climb over barricades,
pressing Beatles photographs to the sky.

Stadiums shake,
fans spring off seats,
innocence shouting out,
weeping, passionate faces,
lights flashing,
cameras clicking,
snapping a new voice:
                        Beatlemania.

A. J. P. Molloy

HELP!

Sliding over
ice cream mountains,
twisted blood and snow scarves
flap out, brushing
an exploding pastel blue rolled sky.

Skis slither
around pianos
dug in snow.

Guitars shuffle fluffed ice:
spades digging holes
in the frozen canvas of earth.

Voices flush over
a gallery of white shadows:
buried wreckages in lost blizzards,
sealing indexes of stories
under ice blankets.

A. J. P. Molloy

Sgt. Pepper's Lonely Hearts Club Band

Swirling rainbow skies
mirrored images of the mystic:
Psychedelic vision.
Storms of possibility
cracked into reality.

Summer of Love:
listening to colours of dreams.
spinning and tumbling,
in washing machines of rainbows.

Travelling in yellow busses,
surfing on clouds.
Rolled up a magical mystery tour,
in circles of flowers
burning under feet.

A concrete statue
pretended to be serious
alone on the hill.
Tears burn cheeks
as fire echoed marmalade
drips down behind.

We breathed rainbows,
shifted colours,
turning shades inside the self,
planned a future
with plasticine wrist watch hands.

We were not afraid to laugh:
A mouth opens
letting out butterflies.
Fluttering rainbows tickle by
twisting up into the roof of the ocean.

A. J. P. Molloy

Andrew Molloy, Age 33
Sydney, Australia

The poems by A. J. P. Molloy were previously published at
http://www.beatles.net/ a part of
http://www.AustralianMedia.com/
Reprinted with permission.

Till There Was You

I just finished seeing Paul on the Arts and Entertainment Channel last night. He was playing in Red Square in Moscow. So many memories flashed by. It is hard for me to watch anything Beatles-related anymore without crying just a little. My entire life was, and still is, Beatles-centered, starting from sixth grade and now well into my fifties!

My sister and I fell in love with the Beatles right after seeing them on the Ed Sullivan Show. That night changed our lives forever. We bought every magazine in sight if it had even had the tiniest photo of them. We were lucky enough to have parents who allowed us to plaster our walls from top to bottom with pictures, even with Beatles wallpaper! I still have several pieces of it left forty years later. My seventh grade teacher was British; how cool was *that,* being able to hear his beautiful accent! He even let us paste Beatle pictures inside our desks!

We spent most of our early teens doing crazy things like waking up in the morning and facing East and pledging allegiance to the Beatles! We had a song we also sang every morning: "We love you Beatles, oh yes we do, we love the things you say and do, when you're not near to us, we're blue, oh, Beatles, we love you!"

When *A Hard Day's Night* came out, we decided that we had to see it more than once, and more than twice. My sister and I and two of our girlfriends went downtown on the train every morning for a week and "lived" at the Woods Theater. We brought our breakfast and lunch with us in brown bags. Each day we sat and watched the movie four or five times and then rode back on the train. I believe we hit an all-time record of twenty times that week alone! I think I'm now up to 45 viewings in total, but who's counting…

When the Beatles first went on tour, my parents were not sure they wanted their two young daughters to see this mop-headed group, but they knew there was no stopping us. We used my dad's banking connections to get third-row seats at the Chicago Amphitheater. Back then, we spent $5.50 on a ticket and we thought we were big stuff because we had spent SO MUCH! That night was our first taste of seeing them up close. My sister pulled off her glasses really quickly when Paul turned to face us, just in case he might look directly at her and think she was cute!

In the following years, we saw them many more times – including twice in the same day at Comiskey Park! We had 2:00 p.m. tickets and 5:00 p.m. tickets. Our parents came along and sat behind us, because they had to see for themselves what all the ruckus was about. They later complained that they couldn't hear the band because of all the screaming. We said we didn't care, we just wanted to see them! We could always hear them on the records.

In 1966, the Beatles came back again and there we were again, back in the third row at the Amphitheater, sobbing our eyes out, knowing that this might be the last time we would ever see them perform together. Sadly, it was.

For the next twenty years I chased all over the country, flying to different arenas to see their solo concerts. First, it was to see Paul and Wings. We probably saw that concert five times. We were so darn jealous of Linda being up there with him. Why couldn't he have married *me*?? George did some concerts; there he was with Ravi Shankar, so mystical, so sincere, so gentle. Then, on to Ringo and his All-Starr Band. How cute he was with his singing and admitting that he is not the best at the keyboard.

As we entered "adulthood," my life still focused on the Beatles. I had converted my fiancé to Beatlemania and our wedding music included three Beatles songs. How could anyone get married without *Till There Was You*?

In 2002 my husband and I saw Paul in Chicago, Phoenix, Los Angeles and Las Vegas. He was at the MGM and we managed to see him on Friday and Saturday. Why should we save our money for the mortgage payment? Seeing Paul takes priority! Then it was on to Phoenix last March for another tour. This time, I wasn't settling for anything past the first ten rows. We went to a scalper and paid a price that no one in their right mind would pay, but we did. It was worth every penny. And, to pass on my love for them, I even splurged on tickets for the whole family. My three sons are now Beatle converts and try to make their own generation aware of the best band of all time.

There is just one more 'slight' indication that I am an addicted, lifelong Beatles fan. I have a museum in my home that is a collection of my memorabilia from the last forty years! It is my comfort zone, my place to go for memories and my place to show my family and friends just what the Beatles have meant to me.

Terie Slugocki, Age 51
Scottsdale, Arizona

On the following pages are some photographs of my personal Beatles museum.

My collection includes several pieces of Beatles wallpaper from 1964, the Beatles dolls, bubble-gum cards, calendars, a bracelet, a "Beatles Fun Kit" and a "Beatles Punch-out Kit." I have all of their original 45s, albums and magazine covers. I still have the original ticket stub from each time I saw *A Hard Day's Night* in the movie theater! I also have some recently-issued collector's items, such as the limited edition "newspaper taxi" cookie jar from a couple of years ago. The most treasured item in my collection? That's easy! My autographed picture of Paul!

In the photo below, I am holding up a piece of Beatles wallpaper.

In this photo, I am holding a "Beatles Fun Kit" and a "Beatles Punch-out Kit."

Terie Slugocki, Age 51
Scottsdale, Arizona

A Young Fan Looks Back

I wasn't around in the 1960s. Not even the 1970s. I was born in 1980 and still managed to "find" the Beatles.

My parents weren't Beatles fans. Well, I don't know for sure about my dad – he died when I was young – but I'm certain my mother never owned a Beatles album because she never mentioned them to me. I sort of "found" them on my own. I always saw their pictures in my history textbooks so I thought, "They must be important. Why not give 'em a try?"

I went down to a local used record shop and I was disappointed that they didn't have any used Beatles CDs. I asked the clerk why they didn't have them and he just laughed and said, "Are you kidding, son? Nobody gives up their Beatles albums," and laughed again. I decided to buy a new Beatles CD, even though I didn't have much money. I was too young to get a job, so I had only my allowance to buy the things I wanted. I didn't even know if I would like their music. I know that girls were initially attracted to their looks but for me to like them, I had to hear the music.

What happened when I finally heard their music? Wow! I can't even describe it. Keep in mind, I was pretty young. I was not used to this type of music. I don't have to describe '80s music to you. You know what was popular and played on the radio. Songs like Toni Basil's *Mickey* were the types of songs offered to us '80s kids. In my opinion, *Mickey* can never compare to *Michelle*. Nothing can compare to any Beatles songs.

Oh, I never did finish telling you about my attempt to own a Beatles CD. Well, after going from the used music store containing no Beatles albums, I wandered into another music store and was overwhelmed by the many albums they sold. How was I to pick one? I didn't know one from the other. I was impressed by the artistic cover of *Revolver*, but thought that I should start with their early stuff, so perhaps *Help!* or *Please Please Me*. I didn't learn much in school but I did learn never to judge a book by its cover. As uninteresting and odd as it looked, I remembered that advice and chose the *White Album*. Out of all the albums I could have started with, what did I do? Purchased the *White Album*...and loved it.

The day I bought it, I ran back to my house and put it in my CD player. I didn't have many friends, so there was nobody for me to invite over to listen to my new CD. My mother heard the music and came in my room only to tell me to turn it down. She had no interest, just as I had thought. So I listened to my CD by myself, but I was happy. I didn't have the company of friends or my mother, but I did have with me thirty of the most brilliant songs I'd ever heard...well, actually, twenty-nine brilliant songs, plus *Wild Honey Pie*.

I listened to that album in the morning, ran home from school and listened to it more. I didn't care about watching TV or listening to the radio; all I needed was my *White Album*. Soon my *White Album* turned into the "black album." I took it with me everywhere and listened to it so much that it became really dirty.

I don't know why I took it everywhere. I didn't have a portable CD player but it felt good just knowing they were *with* me. Remember, I didn't have too many people in my life but that was okay. I had the music of the Beatles. This may sound dumb, but their music became my best friend. If I was sad or happy, I'd turn to their music because I really had nobody else to turn to. I know their music couldn't give me advice, but it was soothing and comforting. Either way, it was all I had. But trust me, I wouldn't have traded that album for anything. I eventually bought every Beatles album and even some posters. To this day, my favorite album is still the *White Album*.

And as impossible as it may seem, I've even grown to appreciate *Wild Honey Pie*.

Allen, Age 23

The Night That Changed My Life

It was a bitter cold, winter night…a Sunday night in February, and my family and I were getting ready to sit down and watch the Ed Sullivan Show at 8 p.m. We always watched Ed Sullivan because, as a variety show, it had a little bit of something for everyone in the family to enjoy. Little did I know that on this particular night my life was going to change forever!

I was ten years old, soon to be eleven. I wasn't quite a teenager yet so I wasn't into the latest trends or into music of any kind. I was still playing with Barbie dolls and playing Candy Land. But that night, four boys from Liverpool – four strange-looking boys from a place I'd never even heard of – were on the Ed Sullivan Show. I watched their first number, mesmerized by their totally foreign look and sound. I was captivated by these new sights and sounds. Later on in the hour they came back to perform again. I was fascinated watching them. Little did I know then the impact these four lads would have on me!

The next day at school, everyone was talking about these four boys, their clothes, their hair, their accents. But I wasn't completely hooked yet. In fact, when my birthday came around in March, one of my friends bought me *Meet the Beatles* as a birthday present and I was disappointed! I had been hoping for new clothes for my Barbie doll, not this album. But I put that record on the turntable and listened to that strange music and stared at that stark, black and white album cover and became hooked. I fell in love with Paul McCartney then, my first-ever crush on a male. Those soulful eyes and cherubic face just had the most jarring effect on me. John intrigued me as well but he looked like he could be tough and mean and was somewhat intimidating to an eleven-year-old. Besides, he was *taken* already. George never seemed to smile and seemed rather foreboding. Ringo, although cute in an odd sort of way, just didn't appeal to my heart the way Paul did.

When *A Hard Day's Night* came out that summer, I realized then that I was about to embark on a love affair that has so far lasted forty years, and shows no signs of letting up. I bought every magazine that had an article on the Fab Four and lovingly made scrapbooks for all those articles. My hard-earned allowance would now be spent entirely on Beatles albums, 45s, and whatever I could get my hands on.

Now fast forward forty years. These days, I always listen to music in the dark with headphones. The other night I was feeling very sad and emotional over a movie I'd just seen in the theater. I pulled out some Beatles CDs, put my headphones on, turned out the lights and listened to the CDs in total darkness.

The first one I played was *With the Beatles* (the British version of *Meet the Beatles*) and listening to those very first songs brought back such unbelievable memories. I was totally transported back in time. Suddenly I was back in my family's first apartment on Jerome Avenue in the Bronx. I could picture every tiny detail of the apartment. I was transported right back to Sunday night, February 9, 1964. I was back in front of the TV watching the Ed Sullivan Show, and hearing and seeing those four strange-looking Englishmen for the first time.

Listening to the album brought back all the incredible memories from 1964. Then I remembered 1965 and 1966 and the Shea Stadium concerts and the summers I spent at Shorehaven, a beach club located on the Bronx side of the Long Island Sound. I remembered my friends and I taking our transistor radios up to the sun deck and listening to all that wonderful Beatles music. I remembered our crush on a lifeguard named Bill who was a Paul McCartney look-alike. We used to pretend to drown ourselves in the pool on a regular basis whenever Bill was on duty.

Oh, to go back to those innocent days!

I still have that first album, *Meet the Beatles*. The edges of the record cover are worn, as are the grooves of this album I can no longer play because turntables have become passé. But my love of the Beatles, their music and everything they represent has endured. Who knew, on that cold, winter night back in 1964, that my life would be changed forever!

Susan Cohen, Age 50
New York, New York

A Tale From The Land Of
The Rising Sun

The new *Let It Be...Naked* has made me remember a lot of things. The first Beatles film I saw was *Let It Be*. I remember I was shocked that they were laughing and sometimes quarreling in the film. I was surprised to find they are really human after all.

In Japan, during the late '60s and even early '70s, there were no TV programs or videos about the Beatles that we could buy. Their LP records were big hits, but public media like TV and radio did not like using them, as Japanese society thought the Beatles to be the symbol of rebellion.

I and all my friends were moved by their music. Their music had something really hard and beautiful – just like diamonds – that stimulated our young minds. The Beatles showed us how to live, how to think, and how to express ourselves as humans. They became our god.

We thought the Beatles to be like our god and then we were surprised when we would see them move, laugh, and talk like humans. *Let It Be* was a sad movie, but it was the real story of our god at the time. What we saw in the film was not pleasant, but it was real.

Let It Be...Naked showed me that the Beatles were like the rest of us humans who try to revise our history. But the songs they produced are beyond the human arts for me. Their impact on me will never change. Their music is like a star, the moon, or the sun. They are always there and can never change.

When John passed away and when George died, a part of my heart also disappeared each time. I loved them as people and I miss them. I also loved them as gods, and their songs were my shining diamonds, and they will never disappear.

Mr. Takeshi Uchiyama
Tokyo, Japan

A Dream Fulfilled

I've had a love affair with the Beatles my entire life. Granted, the height of their popularity was over a decade before I was born. However, I've always loved them with the same fervor as any teenager of the 1960s.

I dreamed of dating a young Paul McCartney and of going to all of their concerts. I was insanely jealous of Linda McCartney for a year during my "Paul crush," but there was no way that a fifteen-year-old would ever stand a chance to be his girlfriend.

My biggest Beatle dream was to go to Liverpool and that dream came true in the summer of 2003. I got to spend three glorious days in Liverpool, a city that is now one of my favorite places in the whole world. Just being in Liverpool made me feel so close to the band that meant so much to me as a teen in the early '90s. Their music was my solace as I struggled through the trials and tribulations of adolescence. It was my personal pilgrimage to Mecca (Macca) and was a trip that I will never forget.

Many of my companions on the trip laughed at my insistence on having my picture taken next to the Penny Lane street sign or going to the Cavern Club twice. They did not understand that this was the only way that I could connect with a time that I was born too late to experience, but have always tried to experience in any way that I could.

Melida Heien, Age 25
Chapel Hill, North Carolina

I Had A Feeling

It's nearly impossible for me to express the amount of joy – both in terms of size and frequency – that the Beatles and their music have brought me "in my life." For me, it's always been about chasing *that feeling* you get from listening to their music and seeing them express their unbridled joy for life in movies like *A Hard Day's Night*. I think that's what it's about for me. I hear and see them do that and wish that I could do it, too!

Wanting to feel more often and more intensely the wonderful and liberating feeling of really *being* a Beatle is probably the thing that motivated me to form a band called "On the Air" that performed Beatles songs exclusively, and to eventually start my own Beatles fan club back in 1995.

The club has since faded away, but not before we had some really fantastically *fun* events including a performance in February 1998 by the tribute band, "The Invasion." They decided to replicate the Beatles' first US concert at the Washington Coliseum (co-hosted by the late WWDC deejay, Carrol James). There was another concert event featuring the excellent young tribute band from Atlanta, "The Roaches." They were joined by the amazingly talented and under-appreciated part of Beatles lore, Roy Young, who performed with the "Fab Three" and Pete Best for several weeks in Hamburg in the spring of '62. Roy Young has the most incredible stories to tell.

In between all that, I've had many incredible moments with a few other Beatle people or celebrities. These moments include being invited backstage to personally meet Sir George Martin on his recent *Sergeant Pepper* speaking tour; seeing Sonny Bono smile as he listened to our band play; having lunch with Walter Shenson only a year or so before his passing; opening for Joey Molland of Badfinger;

briefly meeting Ringo at Tower Records; and sitting second row, center, at Paul's '89 tour (where unquestionable mutual eye contact was made!)

As I reflect on all those great Beatle memories, the one that easily stands out the most in my mind was one lucky day when my best friend Chris and I finally got the chance to *feel* just a bit like what it must have been like to *be* the Beatles on stage!

It was March 1991 at an annual Beatlefest convention in New Jersey. The year before, Chris had taken me to my very first convention. I was blown away by everything, but especially affected by the sound-alike contest where, as a solo artist or a duo, you get to perform one Beatles song for several judges, with the eight selected finalists getting the chance to repeat their performance in the main hall in front of about 2,000 people that same evening.

Driving home from that first convention, I vowed to return next year, ready to kick butt on a song in the hopes of making it to the finals and "getting to be a Beatle," if only for just a moment. I was just an okay guitar player but was more confident about my voice, which I thought sounded better than most of the performers I'd heard that day.

The only problem was that Chris, a total non-musician at the time, wanted to get in on the act, too. Throughout the year, he kept on pestering me about us doing a song together, to which I replied that if he were serious, he'd better be ready to practice so that we wouldn't embarrass ourselves. As it turned out, he *was* serious and we *did* practice! And lucky for us, there was a perfect song to select: *I Should Have Known Better*.

The song was perfect because the recording features a double-tracking of the lead vocal. This meant that Chris and I would both sing it (easily in both our ranges) but not have to harmonize (simply impossible for him at that time).

115

It also featured a simple instrument (harmonica) that, with just a little bit of practice, Chris could conceivably pull off for that one song.

And so we bought the harmonica. I figured out how to play the song and taught it to him, and he practiced his butt off for several weeks before the convention. During our rehearsals, we were inspired to memorize the "Hey, who's that little old man?!" dialogue from the opening train car scene in *A Hard Day's Night*. We thought this might endear us to the judges, potentially improving our chances of getting into the finals (our wildest dream).

Needless to say, we were nerve-wracked that Saturday before the audition. If I remember correctly, we were the very first to audition for the finals and it did seem a bit forced when we went into our little skit. But once we got going with the song, it felt pretty good and I was happy that we were finished and could relax for a few hours until they announced the finalists.

Not sure of our chances – did we stink or were we perhaps not too bad? – we returned to the sound-alike room later that afternoon to await the judges' decision and it didn't take long to hear, as they read the list, "The first finalists are Chris and Jorge." Everyone in the room could hear a very loud "YEAH!!!"

After all the finalists were announced, we were told to be at the main stage at 6:45 p.m. (which was about two hours later). We were flying high and lifted ourselves even higher with a huge cup of coffee that we didn't really need. We then rehearsed a few more times and agreed that we were just going to enjoy the moment. For just a few minutes of our lives we were going to let ourselves feel like we *were* Beatles!

And that's just what we did. When they announced our duo (we were the second or third to perform), we strutted onto the stage, the sound man plugged in my guitar and, once again, we went into our little train car act (to which many in the audience immediately started shouting out the lines along with us!) It was a great way to shake the nerves off.

And then we really let it fly.

With the guitar and harmonica intro and the first line, "I....." you could feel the audience feeding off of our energy. Bopping up and down in my best John Lennon impersonation, I had no other thought on my mind besides, "Wow, this is awesome!"

Perhaps we 'should have' been focusing more on our performance, as it was not without mistakes. Specifically, I remember hitting a "C" chord instead of an "E minor" (or something like that) and, upon hearing the resulting sound, audibly uttering into the mic a confessional "Whoops!" which merited some laughs from the audience.

Later, Chris 'inverted' his harmonica solo a bit, but was just as willing to take full responsibility for the obvious blunder (somewhat more prominent than mine) with his own confessional admission – "Whoa!!" – directly into the mic.

But it didn't matter. Finishing the song with the outro line, "You love me too," over and over, we could hear the audience start to roar with an approval that said, "We know you guys weren't perfect, but we loved you anyway!"

As the crowd cheered, we bowed and gleefully left the stage to make way for the next act. We were in Beatles heaven! And though we didn't win, place or show in the contest, later that evening, while hanging out in the hotel bar, we received countless comments of praise from grateful strangers. That came as quite a surprise to both of us, though we soaked it up for everything it was worth.

Since that special year at Beatlefest, Chris and I have performed a few more times together in the contest, singing

From Me to You (also with harmonica, though also with *harmonies,* which Chris finally caught on to); *Thank You Girl* (the same formula); and *I'm Only Sleeping, Anthology II* version. We even made it to the finals again once or twice and it was always a blast.

But, just as with one's first time experiencing the Beatles, there was something special about that first time. And the fact is, there's no way (except for perhaps winning the darn contest) that it could have been any more *perfectly joyful* for both of us, which is the best description I can give of *that feeling* that I've tried to capture and hold onto before, during, and ever since.

Sadly, those moments are fleeting, but somehow I'm always able to recapture them, through – and because of – being in the company of others who feel the same way that I do about the Beatles. For the joy that the Beatles bring is even better when shared!

Jorge Bernardo, Age 39
Arlington, Virginia

A Love Story

Dedicated to the memory of Carl Hoskisson

I first stumbled across the Beatles around the time the movie *Backbeat* was released. After seeing it the first time, I had to return and see it time and time again. I even went as far as entering a competition and winning tickets to see the film. This was the beginning of my life as a Beatles fan.

In 1998 the opportunity arose for me to move from Sheffield to Liverpool and I grabbed it with both hands! (What Beatles fan in their right mind wouldn't?) This was around the time of the annual Beatles festival that takes place in Liverpool each August. At the festival, I participated in all the Beatle tributes on Mathew Street, including going to the Cavern to hear Beatle tribute bands and seeing the statues of John Lennon and the Beatles in Cavern Walks.

In 2000, I met my boyfriend, Carl. He and his father were very keen on the Beatles. When Carl and I moved in together, his dad gave us a large mirror to hang on the lounge wall. Upon it was a picture of John Lennon and the lyrics to *Imagine*. He also gave me a signed photo of Allan Williams, the Beatles' first manager, along with complimentary tickets for a concert by Beatle tribute bands and for the annual convention taking place at the Adelphi Hotel in Liverpool. The atmosphere at that convention was electric! I had never felt the likes of it before. It was truly another world to me.

At the 2001 Beatles festival, we saw many more Fab Four tribute bands. I never realised there could be so many! We also had a fantastic opportunity to meet a lot of people associated with the Beatles, such as Astrid Kirchherr, Allan Williams, Pete Best, Julia Baird and many more.

On the August Bank Holiday Monday in 2002, Carl and I once again headed into Liverpool City Centre for the annual Beatles convention to watch as many different bands as we could and to try to catch Pete Best playing for the one and only time at the festival as a tribute to George Harrison, who'd passed away the previous November. This event was sponsored by our local radio station. We planned to get there early, but many others had the same idea and had already begun to gather around the stage. Carl knew I wanted to be as close to the stage as possible and did everything possible to get us as close as he could. I still, to this day, cannot think of a more perfect way to round off a perfect weekend. Words really do fail me.

Much of my collection of Beatles memorabilia is due to Carl's efforts. He always went out of his way to get things for me, such as the time in 2001 that Carl managed to catch up with Paul McCartney after Paul had just finished a book signing session for his book, *Blackbird Singing.* Carl actually *got* Paul's autograph for me!!! Carl also took me to the Liverpool Philharmonic Hall to see *A Hard Day's Night,* the one Beatles film I had not yet seen.

The one thing I must say is that throughout the highs and the lows of my life, the Beatles have always been there. Whenever Carl and I were spending some quality time together, we would have the Beatles' most romantic songs on in the background. When I passed my exams at college, we celebrated with a drink or two and upbeat Beatles songs.

The Beatles were the ones to whom I turned at the lowest point of my life in December 2002, when Carl died tragically and suddenly. I turned to the Beatles now, just as I had in the happy times. On the day of his cremation, Carl's parents arranged for *In My Life* to be played as everyone entered the chapel. It was so appropriate from my point of view, as there always will be places that I will see as I travel around Liverpool that will bring back fond memories of the happy times we shared. As we exited the chapel, *Good Night* was playing. To this day, it still breaks my heart when I hear it because that day it was as if Carl were saying his goodbye.

I am now, just one year later, slowly getting back on my feet. I take each day as it comes. When I wake up each day I know that no matter what mood I'm in, I have Carl – who, let's face it, is now in pretty good company: John and George! – watching over me, and I know I will find a Beatles song to match my mood.

Donna Stokes, Age 32
Liverpool, England

Remembering The Beatles' First Visit To America

It was two weeks before my seventh birthday when the Beatles arrived in New York City on February 7, 1964. It was a winter Friday afternoon. As young as I was, it is a day I will never forget.

I remember that my older cousin Gary was watching me until my parents came home from work. Gary told me to be sure to watch Ed Sullivan that Sunday night, which we always did anyway, given that we were only able to get three channels on our black and white television set. Ed Sullivan's variety show was a weekly ritual. Gary went on to explain, "The Beatles are going to be on Ed Sullivan!" I remember asking him, "Who are the Beatles?" and Gary replied, "They are a rock and roll band from England." Okay, but it didn't mean much to me that day.

On Sunday, February 9, 1964, my family and I watched the Ed Sullivan Show. From that moment on, I was hooked!!!! The Beatles were, and still are, the best rock and roll band on the planet!

With 73 million Americans watching that night, the Beatles gave our country a much needed boost following President Kennedy's assassination only two and a half months earlier. They really helped to lift our country out of its sadness and mourning. To us kids, the Beatles were the best thing since sliced bread! Their music always brings me back to the joy of childhood.

My own children ask me why I love the Beatles so much and my standard reply is, "Their music brings me back to a wonderful time in my life."

Stan Taraska, Age 46
Ipswich, Massachusetts

The Discovery

I dug around blindly in the shoebox at the back of the station wagon. I made a face as I pulled out a tape by some jazz instrumental group that my mother liked to listen to. I really didn't care for that kind of "old people" music.

Looking back on it, I don't know why I felt the urge that day to look through my parents' cassette collection, other than the fact that I was bored and it seemed like a good idea at the time. All I know is that one choice changed my life more than I could have ever imagined. It was the precise moment in the late summer of 1995 in the Snowy Range Mountains of Wyoming that I found the *White Album*.

I'd nearly given up on finding anything decent when I pulled out cassette one of *The Beatles*. It had been years since I listened to their music. I remembered pointing at the four men on the black and white cassette cover and guessing their names when I was about five or six. Now this cassette intrigued me enough to investigate further. Grabbing my Sony Walkman, I slid the tape in place and pushed the little arrow – and my life – into 'play' mode.

The loud explosion of the plane noise in *Back in the USSR* hit me like a tidal wave. I listened all the way through the first side, enthralled with what I heard. When the tape clicked to a stop, I glanced around to see if anyone had witnessed my discovery. No one was in the vicinity, and I scrambled out of the car and walked briskly down the dirt path, until I came to a lonely meadow where I could listen in peace. In the empty open air and solace of the remote mountains, I played the cassette over and over until the batteries in my player died and the sun was setting in the sky.

When I finally returned to our camping area, my parents asked me where I had been. I wanted so desperately to keep this secret to myself, though I did not understand why. This thing I had was too important to waste while trifling with others. I told my parents I had been on a walk and got lost.

It was not totally a lie. I lost my old self that day. I was transformed into a new person. I matured greatly in an extremely short span of time. To this day, I still cannot fully explain what happened to me. The experience was mind-blowing. To put it in perspective: I had every piece of knowledge in my brain ripped out and newly formulated; I found a new purpose in life, and thought about ideas. I think that was the most intense part of my experience. Until that day, I had been a normal eleven-year-old on a family vacation. After that, I was a young adult – fully capable of seeing the world not just as a mythic thing, but as a reality.

Many people can mark the day they 'came of age' or the time of their realization. It is a time when you can grasp, however slightly, the concept of the world and the universe. It is a stage where you realize everything around you, and its purpose, its meaning. The Beatles catapulted me into complex understanding, and gave me a sense of myself in the context of my environment. Since that moment, there is not a day that goes by that I do not listen to their music, or reflect on their songs. To me, the Beatles were the medium that introduced me to all the endless possibilities in the world.

"You say you want a revolution...well, you know, we all wanna change the world."
–John Lennon/Paul McCartney

© Julia Cryne, Age 19
Omaha, Nebraska

The Concert Remembered

I gaze at the concert poster on my door,
And find myself sucked into a vortex of memories.
Suddenly I am there–
Within the moving, sweating ocean of bodies.

Blue and yellow lights cascade around me–
An aurora in the guise of a light show.
The thundering boom and crash of the drums
Compound in my ears.

Happiness overflows in a high tide in my being.
His hand is close as I reach toward him–
My fingers gently graze Ringo's two-dimensional face.

*This poem was written about my memories of a Ringo and
his All-Starr Band concert I went to... 6th row!!*

© Julia Cryne, Age 17
Omaha, Nebraska

The Dark Horse Has Fallen

The Dark Horse has fallen,
His silence resounds–
The aching empty feeling
Toward the hollow abyss creeps–
While My Guitar Gently Weeps.

You've surpassed the Art of Dying,
Shown the world the light
That comes from religious devotion–
The tears from mine eye still seeps–
While My Guitar Gently Weeps.

All Things Must Pass
Yet all the words that this world would bring
Cannot escape the loss of my heart;
And the mountain of despair heaps–
While My Guitar Gently Weeps.

Written in the aftermath of George Harrison's death.

© Julia Cryne, Age 17
Omaha, Nebraska

Rock And Roll Music

I grew up in New Orleans in the Sixties. Those were the days when radio airwaves were dominated by a format called Top Forty. It was also a time when local stations across the country played what they wanted to play. Disc jockeys were not handcuffed by play lists dictated by a few programmers from national headquarters. This led to regional hits and stations that had their own local flavor. In New Orleans, Top Forty meant a mix of pop, rock and good ole New Orleans R&B. In 1963, it would not have been unusual for my favorite station, WTIX, to play *Dominique* by the Singing Nun, followed by the Kingsmen's *Louie Louie* and Fats Domino's *Walking to New Orleans*. Radio was adventurous, and I loved it.

And then, in 1964, it got even better. One afternoon in early January, while riding home on the school bus, I heard something different and exciting. From the opening chords of *I Want to Hold Your Hand*, I was hooked. I became a Beatles fan for life. And although WTIX continued to play a wide variety of music, the station made sure it gave listeners a heavy dose of Beatles songs. And it wasn't just singles, like *She Loves You* and *Please Please Me*. Ringo was very popular, so *I Wanna Be Your Man* blasted through speakers all over town. And while stations across the nation retained their uniqueness, nearly all had one thing in common. They played lots of Beatles.

1964 was also the year I began buying records. Prior to that time, I "borrowed" singles and albums from my older sisters. I still have their copy of *The Coasters' Greatest Hits* and have no intention of ever giving it back. The first album I purchased was *Meet the Beatles.* Although I played that record hundreds of times on a cheap turntable, it still sounds great when I play it now on my vintage Beatles record player. The scratches on the vinyl and the low fidelity of the old tube record player only enhance the experience.

In addition to listening to the music, I always read the liner notes and took notice of who wrote the songs. On the Coasters' album, nearly all of the songs were written by Jerry Lieber and Mike Stoller, the "guiding geniuses" who rehearsed the group, mapped out arrangements and supervised the recording sessions. On the Beatles albums, nearly all of the songs were written by John Lennon and Paul McCartney, who were members of the group. The fact that all of those great tunes were written by band members further impressed me because, prior to the Beatles, very few recording artists wrote their own songs.

And then one night in February 1964, I finally got to see the Beatles perform and witness firsthand the excitement of Beatlemania. Sure, it was just on TV, but those black and white images are forever imbedded in my mind. For three Sunday evenings in a row, Ed Sullivan brought the Beatles and those screaming girls into my home.

As the Sixties rolled on, the Beatles kept releasing records on a pace similar to that of US manned space flights. And while each space flight had different goals and programs, each new Beatles disc had different sounds and textures. In December 1965, the Beatles released a double A-side single, *We Can Work It Out* b/w *Day Tripper*, and an incredible album, *Rubber Soul*. NASA put up two space flights, Gemini VII and Gemini VI, which became the first vehicles to rendezvous in space. During 1966, while Project Gemini prepared astronauts for the next phase with complex rendezvous, docking and space walk missions, the Beatles began readying themselves for their next phase with innovative use of instruments and complex studio techniques on *Paperback Writer*, *Rain* and *Revolver*.

In late 1968, the Beatles put out the *White Album* and NASA put three men in lunar orbit aboard Apollo VIII. It was an exciting time. In July of 1969, NASA put a man on the moon, and made it look easy. In October of that year, the Beatles released *Abbey Road*, an album highlighted by great individual songs on side one and a seamless medley on side two. They also made it look easy. Then, in April 1970, Paul announced he was quitting the Beatles. Shortly thereafter, NASA nearly lost the crew of Apollo XIII. It was the end of an era or two. Yes, the individual Beatles put out solo albums and there were a few more moon flights, but it wasn't the same. George was right: All Things Must Pass.

By the time I started law school in 1977, the Beatles were still a part of my life, but not to the same degree. I bought the solo albums out of habit, but the excitement was gone. And then, one horrible Monday night in December 1980, John Lennon was gone.

*   *   *   *   *   *   *   *

In 1996, I settled a class action law suit that restored lost pension benefits to a group of retirees. It also brought me a large fee based upon four years of hard work on the case. Rather than go out and buy a Rolex or a Mercedes Benz, I decided to start collecting Beatles records and memorabilia. I contacted dealers advertising in the annual *Goldmine* Beatles issue and, from them, bought the records that became the backbone of my collection.

I quickly developed a fondness for the Beatles' singles and albums on Vee-Jay. When Perry Cox, author of a series of price guides on Beatles records and memorabilia, asked me to write an article on the Vee-Jay releases for an upcoming price guide, I responded with a 2,000 word article. Perry liked the piece and casually mentioned there might be a book in there. After giving it some thought, I decided to write a book about the Beatles' records on Vee-Jay. As soon as the Vee-Jay book came out, people began asking when the Capitol book was coming out. And so I began writing a series of books on the Beatles' American records. It became my specialty area in the wide world of Beatles lore.

In December of 2002, I gained access to a box full of vintage Vee-Jay documents that, under the normal course of events, would have been destroyed decades ago. The most interesting item was a February 1, 1963, telegram from Vee-Jay president Ewart Abner to Concertone Songs that stated, "PLEASE, PLEASE ME BY THE BEATTLES WILL BE RELEASED FEBRUARY SEVEN." At first, I was excited because I now knew the exact release date for the single. And then it hit me. The Beatles first record in America was released on February 7, 1963, exactly one year prior to the group's arrival in America on February 7, 1964. In the back of my mind, I knew there was a book in that. By January, 2003, I made the decision to write a book about the first US visit and the events leading up to it. The following month I came up with the title, *The Beatles Are Coming! The Birth of Beatlemania in America*, and began work on the project. I completed the book by the end of the summer.

When I first saw the Beatles on the Ed Sullivan Show all those years ago, I knew it was a special moment. But I never dreamed that forty years later I'd still remember the event, much less write a book about it.

Bruce Spizer
New Orleans, Louisiana

Bruce Spizer is a first generation Beatles fan and well-known Beatles author/historian. He is considered the leading expert on the group's North American record releases.

A "taxman" by day, Spizer is a board certified tax attorney and certified public accountant. A "paperback writer" by night, he is the author of the critically acclaimed books, *The*

Beatles Records on Vee-Jay, *The Beatles' Story on Capitol Records, Parts One and Two*, *The Beatles on Apple Records*, and *The Beatles Are Coming! The Birth of Beatlemania in America*. His articles have appeared in *Beatlology Magazine*, *Beatlefan*, *Day Trippin'*, *Goldmine* and *American History*. He maintains the popular Beatles collectors' internet site www.beatle.net.

Fab Four Only Feet Away!

When I was at the innocent age of eight, my three older sisters and my brother listened to Beatles music, as my sisters were huge fans of the Beatles. Each sister "chose" one Beatle to idolize. Ringo was not chosen, so I figured I was supposed to like him. So I did. We "played" guitars, drums, and sang in our basement as we tried to imitate them. Our family had a parakeet named Ringo. One day when I came home from school my mother told me that Ringo had died. I was really sad and started crying and then I realized it was the parakeet!

In 1965, for my sister's eighth grade graduation, she got tickets to see the Beatles perform at Comiskey Park, a baseball stadium in Chicago. The two lucky ones who got to go were my older sisters, Vicki and Kathi. Since we lived in Wauconda at that time, my father decided to wait outside for them until the concert was over since it would be too far to drive home and then back again, as Comiskey Park was nearly an hour from our home.

My father, my sister Toni, my brother Steve, and I waited outside Comiskey that night. We waited and heard the massive screams coming from inside the park. To us, it sounded like the concert was already going on. We were waiting behind the steel bars that wrapped around the park. Other people waited as well.

Suddenly, a big, black car pulled into the back of Comiskey Park and drove through an opening in the steel gates not far from where we were standing. The steel gate closed immediately behind this car. People screamed and started to rush over to that area to see what was happening. I tried to gaze over people with my short, little body to get a better look. I did not know what was going on. Who or what was it that got everyone in such an uproar? I heard familiar names being shouted out as four lads exited the car.

I pressed my face in between the bars to get a closer look. No wonder there was yelling and screaming! There they were. It was the "boys" whom I thought were already playing inside! John, Paul, George, and Ringo!

There were the Beatles, whom my sisters and I pretended to imitate. I was seeing the actual faces of the Beatles whose music I "played." They started walking up the ramp into the ballpark about fifty feet in front of us. They waved to the screaming people who were now hanging onto the bars with their arms reaching through them. All the people tried to "touch" the Beatles. I was one of them! "Paul! Paul!" I yelled in my eight-year-old voice. He heard me and he looked at me! "John!" someone else yelled. George had long locks of hair down to his shoulders and "fluffed" it as he looked our way.

When the concert was over we journeyed back home. On our way home, I remember my father telling my sisters who had been inside to see the concert, "The Beatles were only fifty feet away from us!!" Standing outside, we had seen them much closer than they did inside the ballpark! My father, sister, brother and I saw the famous Beatles as close as if they were in our backyard. I still remember it to this day. I will never forget Comiskey Park. It did not have anything to do with baseball that day, yet I will not forget its name because it was where I first saw the Beatles!

Liz Deasey Myers, Age 47
Crystal Lake, Illinois

Beatlemania: Then And Now

I'm twenty-one years old and have been a Beatles fan for as long as I can remember and I have my mother to thank. She was a Beatles fan all her life, beginning at age thirteen when they arrived in 1964 and stirred up hysteria in every young girl's life.

I truly do thank her for exposing me to the Fab Four. I have friends who can't name all four Beatles. They can usually come up with John and Paul after a few minutes of prodding, but George and Ringo? Forget it! While growing up, I always listened to Beatles songs so I found it odd that my friends couldn't sing along with me when we heard them on the radio. My mother didn't force their music on me – well…okay, she did – but *even if I could have escaped* their music, I wouldn't have wanted to. Their music was always on in the house, the car, and was pretty much in my blood. When I was much younger, I really couldn't appreciate the lyrics but I liked the beats of the songs. As I grew up, I listened to more of their albums and eventually I was able to call myself a Beatles fan.

For me, it was as if the Beatles had come around again in the 1990s, and I was given the chance to experience Beatlemania for myself. For me, it began just as it had for so many other girls – I decided who was the cutest and who my favorite was. When I first saw them, it was Ringo, hands down. I felt bad for him being stuck all the way back there on the drums. I don't remember the first Beatles song I ever heard or liked, but I gradually listened to all of their albums. I believe it started with *Sgt. Pepper's Lonely Hearts Club Band*, which was a bit challenging for me at the time as a young teenager. Many of the lyrics didn't make much sense to me at the beginning.

As I got older, I grew even fonder of the Beatles. I started to read about them in all the Beatle books my mom has in the house. My favorite was one of the first that I selected to read, which was all about the "Paul is Dead" craziness. As humorous as it was, I also found it very interesting and compelling. I immediately grabbed my Beatles CDs to search for the supposed clues to his death.

After the books came the films. It was at this point that I changed my mind about who, exactly, was the cutest of the four. It was now Paul. He was always considered to be "the cute one" and was my mom's favorite. As I said earlier, the 1990s gave me a chance to relive Beatlemania so I did what every Beatles fan did in 1964: see *A Hard Day's Night* in the theater! Yes, for the movie's re-release in December 2000, a local theater was showing the film for only a few days and I knew I had to see it on the big screen! It was more amazing than I ever thought it would be.

There I was, eighteen years old, sitting in a theater full of Beatles fans – many of them younger than me – watching the celebrated black and white film filled with the songs, humor and antics for which the lads from Liverpool are remembered. The only difference was that I actually *heard* the dialogue in the film, except for a few words that were hard to decipher due to the boys' beautiful but strong Liverpool accents. My mom told me that when she saw it in 1964 (every time she saw it, that is!) the girls screamed and cried so much that nobody caught one word of the dialogue (but then again, nobody really cared!) They were there to see their idols up close and larger than life. While sitting in the theater in 2000 watching the Beatles and the much-loved "clean old man," I thought to myself, "It can't get any better than this!" But it *did*.

The day I met Paul McCartney is something I will never, ever forget. After waiting in line for over seventeen hours (with my mother and our cousin Susan) to see Paul, and sleeping out overnight on the street in New York City, it was all worth it. Sir Paul was doing a book signing in New York on June 11, 2001, and I knew that IF we were lucky enough to be among the few fans to get inside, I was going to get to speak to him and shake his hand.

How do I say everything I feel about him, his music, and about the Beatles in probably less than thirty seconds?? Today, I'm still asking myself that question. As Paul shook my hand – which was my cue to begin talking – I simply froze and stood there, unable to say one word. I was in complete shock being in front of not only a Beatle, but my favorite Beatle!! Wow, every time I think back to that day when I stood before THE Paul McCartney, I laugh at how I couldn't say anything at all!!

When my mom saw that I was too much in awe to speak, she wasn't about to let my thirty seconds with Paul go to waste. She had already gotten the handshake and talked to him and he had autographed her book. So when I was standing there, stunned and speechless, she said, "Paul, this is my daughter, she's a second-generation Beatles fan!" Paul looked directly up at me, and said, "Hello, Daughter!" with that incredible accent. That's all he said. He looked right at me when he said it. After this direct eye contact with Paul, my mind went even blanker, and I was still unable to say one word to him! When I saw his "Back in the US" concert in 2002 and looked around the packed arena, I kept thinking to myself: I am probably *the only one* in this entire place (unless his kids were there at the Fleet Center that night) to whom Paul has ever said, "Hello, Daughter!"

Another way I experienced Beatlemania for myself in the 1990s was by visiting Liverpool. In 1998 and 1999, my mom, my brother and I went on a tour that took us to London and Liverpool, where we saw every imaginable Beatles site. The Beatles' history and everything I'd always heard and read about came alive for me.

So how did I become such a huge Beatles fan? I guess you can say it was my mother who first introduced me to them, but it was their music that captivated me and drew me to become part of their unbounded circle of admirers. As much as I would give anything to turn back time and experience Beatlemania during the 1960s, I am grateful to have had a chance to relive the experience in my own way. And meeting Paul McCartney in person and shaking his hand isn't *a bad way* to experience Beatlemania!!!!!

I have no doubt that the Beatles will continue to have an effect on young teens (my future children included!) for years to come. Future musicians will be influenced by the Beatles, and their music will always be heard while their legend will continue to live on. I believe that millions of teenagers will experience Beatlemania for themselves, just as I did, each in their own special and unique way, and will realize the brilliance of their music and the importance of their "invasion."

Alyssa Schultz, Age 21
Newton, Massachusetts

A Night I'll Never Forget

I attended the Beatles' last-ever public performance in Liverpool. I think it was late November 1963, and it was at a televised recording of the Saturday night show known as Juke Box Jury. I'd just turned eight and I loved the Beatles. We were lucky to have a famous UK celebrity in the family who was also a friend and contemporary of the Beatles. He was a local Liverpool comedian called Jimmy Tarbuck, and he sported a Beatles haircut. He obtained tickets for me, my mum, and his wife, Pauline, in the upper circle on the first floor, front row, of the Liverpool Empire Theatre.

I remember lots of screams coming from the girls. The Beatles played for only about half an hour. The show was filmed at about 5 p.m. and broadcast later that same evening at about 7 p.m. At one point during the concert, a camera zoomed in on me. I had a packet of sweets in my hand, either pastels or opal fruits (UK candy of the time) and I think that some comment was made about that on TV, but my mother and I are not sure.

The next day a few neighbours knocked at my house to tell my parents that they had seen me on TV. That was a big deal back then...possibly still is. Since then, I have tried to trace the film which was made by the BBC, but to no avail as apparently it has been lost or destroyed, although my local newspaper, *The Liverpool Echo*, did a Beatles feature story not so long ago and did a mini feature on that concert.

Strawberry fields forever...

Mike McLoughlin, Age 48
Liverpool, England

Beatlemania In America: Britain's Revenge For The Boston Tea Party!

In February 1964, I was at the ripe old age of twelve and in the seventh grade when THEY came upon the scene. What an amazing time it was! We were all so captivated by their looks, their music, and everything about them after that mesmerizing appearance on the Ed Sullivan Show.

I recall my friends coming over to watch the show. We had been counting down the hours. We sat grouped around a very small black and white set, ready for those four lads to appear on the screen. My parents sat on the sofa and watched us. THEN, finally, 8 p.m.! Suddenly, there they were – so cute, and that music, and the lyrics, and Paul!! I fell in love with Paul at that instant, and screamed loudest whenever the camera was on him. We pressed our hands against their faces on the screen, as if somehow we could magically touch them. My father was laughing himself silly watching us. It was so very emotional and after it was over, all we could talk about was how wonderful they were, how fantastic the music was, how new and exciting. We felt completely drained and exhilarated at the same time. We wanted to hold onto that night and relive it in our minds over and over.

The next months were all about the four boys from Liverpool. We wanted to speak like they did. We took turns each week being their girlfriend or wife. We were overjoyed when it was our turn to have our favorite Beatle. We made up stories about what we would do if we were really their girlfriends. We spent long hours sitting on the floor in the drugstore, looking at *Sixteen* or *Teen Screen* magazine and pooling our money to buy the latest issue. The centerfold would look lovely in our locker, for us to gaze at and dream.

The Beatles' photos hung on every wall in my room. My mom even bought me a piece of Beatle wallpaper. We had dreams of meeting them, or touching them, or just getting to see them.

That summer, tickets went on sale in advance for *A Hard Day's Night*. Each ticket cost an entire dollar. Considering that movies were 35 or 50 cents then, a dollar seemed like a lot of money. My grandmother gave me the money for both my girlfriend and me to go see it. I rode my bike to the Shore Theater and sat in line in the back alley, waiting for my turn. I hoped they wouldn't sell out. Finally it was my turn to buy my ticket. It was a huge yellow ticket, with a picture of the Beatles and the date of the movie: Wednesday, August 12 at 8 p.m. I was so excited! I raced home with the treasure! We were going to see them on the big screen!

The waiting seemed endless, but finally August 12 arrived. We wolfed down some dinner and literally ran from our homes to the theater, cutting through the projects to get there faster. We met up with other friends and waited in line. We had about two or three hours before the movie would start, but we wanted good seats. We each wore our Beatle sweatshirts. They didn't have Beatle T-shirts back then, so even though it was August, and very hot, we wore our Beatle sweatshirts. We didn't mind the heat...or the fact that our moms made us wear skirts and knee socks!

One of my friends brought her transistor radio to help us pass the time. Finally, the doors opened and everyone poured inside like sand pouring through a funnel. I never did find out what became of the policeman at the door. He disappeared under the crush of us all and was never seen again.

They handed out 8x10 pictures of your favorite Beatle. Of course, I grabbed for Paul. It is rather crumpled...it is hard to hold it still when you are standing and screaming all night.

Then, suddenly, there THEY were on the screen! We stood up and a huge scream emanated from all of us at once. One of my girlfriends actually passed out at the first sight of Paul on the screen. We had to crawl under people to pick her up, along with various pieces of her radio, which had fallen to the floor when she passed out. We dropped her and her radio back into her seat, and resumed our screaming.

We screamed through the entire movie. Nobody said we went to *hear* it! We went to *see* them! We went to see it a second time, in the hopes of hearing some dialogue this time, but we screamed again; screaming was just not something that could be held in. The screams welled up like volcanoes in us until they exploded. We had no voices left after seeing the movie. My dad said that it was one time the party line on our telephone would be happy because I had no voice left to use the phone. To us, the sacrificing of our vocal cords was minor. We had gotten to see the Beatles in a movie!

When school began, we all carried Beatle notebooks, binders and fresh pictures to hang on lockers or keep inside a book to stare at whenever the teachers weren't looking. My mom gave me the movie novelization. We sat in homeroom and read it. It was like reliving the movie all over again. We practiced trying to write like they did, and we even ate like they did. The boys tried to dress like them, and even though long hair was not allowed in school, they grew bangs and combed them down.

My friends and I didn't get to see the Beatles live that year. Our moms said that twelve was too young. In fact, the day of the Beatles concert was the only time my mom ever drove me to school. Since the radio station was playing Beatles music all day, we took a transistor radio to school. Radios were not allowed in school. My girlfriend actually brought a rope and tied it around the radio, and we set it on the window ledge during homeroom. We couldn't hear much, but it made us feel close to them, just knowing they were outside that window. My grandmother bought me Beatle boots, which I wore until they fell apart. My mom bought me a Lennon cap, which I still wear.

It was a very magical year. Perhaps over time we get more nostalgic over it than it actually was, but it was a year to remember. I, for one, will never forget it.

Betty Taucher, Age 51
Mentor, Ohio

1964 revisited

the melodies echo in my mind

creating visions of my youth,

in troubled times I am not alone,

words reverberate and I can sing again.

the spirit of the music is always there,

to hold, sustain and cherish,

makes me cry, makes me happy,

reminder of a time forever kept,

·   softening the scratches in life,

a magic soothing sound,

a starburst of joy to radiate the dark places of my soul.

Betty Taucher, Age 51
Mentor, Ohio

Before He Was Fab

Back in 1963, while living in Benton, Illinois, we had a friend named Gabe McCarty who was the leader of a small four-man band known as the Four Vests. My wife and I frequently went to hear them play on Saturday nights. The band occasionally practiced at our house.

Louise Harrison Caldwell also lived in Benton and had been trying to promote her little brother's band – the Beatles – though not too successfully, in America.

The Beatles took a holiday (vacation) from their work in the fall of 1963. George was planning to come to America to visit his sister, Louise, and bring his friend Ringo with him. Ringo, upon learning that Lou was trying to promote the Beatles in the US, decided he wasn't going to come, so George brought his brother Peter with him instead.

Louise contacted Gabe McCarty and asked if he would come to her home and meet her little brother, as they had things in common. Gabe did, and asked George to come to the Eldorado VFW (Veterans of Foreign Wars) Club where they were playing on Saturday night. He also invited my wife and me to join them, which we did. George had been asked in advance to play guitar, but declined. At one point during the evening, Gabe had his lead guitarist go over to George and ask him to just fill in while he went to the restroom. The ploy worked and George got up to play.

In those days, bands played to crowds that never really heard anything. They were mainly interested in dancing and drinking beer. When George started to play, everyone stopped what they were doing and listened to the band. It was really something to see. George played a few Chet Atkins and Buddy Holly tunes.

When we learned that the house in which George had stayed in 1963 was slated to be torn down, we and several others bought it in order to keep the memory of his very first visit to the US intact. It is now The Hard Days Nite Bed & Breakfast in Benton, Illinois.

Jim Chady
Benton, Illinois
www.harddaysnitebnb.com

A "Fine" Beginning

I'm 25 years old and am happy to say that the Beatles have been a huge part of my life. I officially declared the Beatles to be my favorite group at the age of ten and have been listening, collecting, and loving ever since.

During college, I was lucky enough to spend time abroad and am proud to say that before the age of 21, I had been to Liverpool (or Mecca, as I call it) twice.

After college, I joined the work force and met a man. Immediately, I felt an attraction to him but found out that he was eighteen years older than me, so I didn't pursue him. One night, he and I ended up out together with a bunch of other people from work. We fell in love over the jukebox. The song that was playing? *I Feel Fine*.

I discovered that he is a huge Beatles fan and even a bigger George Harrison fan. On our first Valentine's Day together, I decided to buy him a shirt from *The Concert for George*. Unfortunately, it didn't arrive on time. Instead, it arrived on February 25th, George's birthday. This past summer at a Beatles festival, we had the opportunity to meet George's older sister, Louise. She loved hearing our story.

Corri Glydon, Age 25
Uxbridge, Massachusetts

Paul Was In A Group Before Wings?

I was driving home from the store a few weeks ago and while listening to the radio I heard the deejay spouting off a bunch of upcoming concert dates. The last thing he announced was that Paul McCartney would be appearing in Indianapolis on October 5, 2002.

It seems that I have the worst luck when it comes to hearing about concerts in time enough to get a ticket, let alone a good seat. But being the Beatlemaniac that I am, I immediately decided that if there were any tickets left, I was going.

I had a chance to see McCartney back in March. I paid $135 to see his show in Atlanta, but I wasn't going to pass up another opportunity to see him, mainly because he was going to be so close to home. When I got home I gave my buddy Ted a call to tell him about the concert. He too is a huge Beatles fan and he told me to put him down for two tickets: one for himself and one for his wife.

I went online and purchased four $55 tickets. (Not exactly the best seats in the house, but, hey, I'd probably pay money to sit underneath the stage for a McCartney concert.) Since I didn't want to be the odd man out, I purchased the fourth ticket for my friend Faith.

Faith is Ted's neighbor and a mutual friend of ours. Although she's never claimed to be a Beatles fan, I figured she was enough of a music fan to appreciate a last chance opportunity to see a Beatle in concert.

I mean, let's be honest, folks. Sir Paul isn't getting any younger.

Plus, I knew a couple of other people who would go if Faith couldn't make it, so I wasn't too worried about the extra ticket going to waste.

I called Faith after I got the tickets and told her about the concert. She said that the date was too far away to know for sure, but that she would like to go if she could make it.

Okay, this is the part of the story where I actually start to make a point, so please bear with me.

Apparently, a couple of days after I told Faith about the concert she had a conversation with her best friend, Shonna. Shonna also happens to be my barber, so I know her fairly well.

The details of this conversation are unknown to me since I wasn't there at the time, but the gist of it was Shonna asking Faith (in my head I imagine this being asked in a very whiney voice), "Why would you wanna go see Paul McCartney?!"

A childish question, but a question a child may ask.

Seeing Paul McCartney in concert is like having a chance to witness a part of history. I am often perplexed as to how people who *claim* to be music fans have no knowledge or appreciation of the impact the Beatles made on the world. It seems the vast majority of people under the age of thirty have no clue that there was actually music recorded before they were born.

Almost every musician from almost every genre has been directly influenced by the Beatles. (Except, of course, for Michael Stipe of R.E.M. He has called Beatles music "elevator music.")

Now, I've never expected everyone to suddenly go out and purchase Beatle CDs and become Beatle fans. But they should at least show a little respect.

Whenever I hear anyone tell me that the Beatles sucked, it makes me think about what it would be like if there were a group of politicians with the same moronic attitude and lack of knowledge, discussing the history of the US presidency on a C-SPAN panel show:

Politician #1: "Gentleman, I would like to state for the record that Thomas Jefferson totally sucked. He wore a white wig that made him look girly and stupid."

Politician #2: "I concur. Not to mention he's all old and dead."

Politician #3: "I agree as well. I can't think of anything cool he did. But do you guys remember Bill Clinton? Now he did some pretty cool stuff."

The point I'm trying to make is that just because half the Beatles are dead and the other half are in their sixties doesn't mean that their cultural influence and musical accomplishments should go unlearned and be forgotten.

The Beatles recorded thirteen albums in a seven-year span. I'd like to see Eminem or Linkin Park even try to come close to doing that. And, in that seven-year span, their music evolved in unprecedented ways. They were the first to experiment with different sounds, like sampling and feedback. The film *A Hard Day's Night* changed the way movies were made. The Beatles made it okay to be different, to grow your hair long and to wear what you wanted. They made rock and roll central in the lives of youths. They shook up the system.

Well, I could go on and on, but I must conclude. This column has already drawn out much longer than I intended it to, and I'm sure that it will do nothing as far as helping to curb the ignorance of my peers.

And, as it turns out, when I went in to get my hair cut the other day Shonna told me that she didn't say anything to Faith about the concert. No matter, though; I was already pissed off. Not specifically at Shonna, though. I could never get too upset with her because she has the ability to make the bald spot on the top of my head even larger than it already is.

Incidentally, I've since been informed by Faith that she will be unable to attend the McCartney concert with us this coming weekend, so I've decided to ask Michael Stipe if he'll join me instead. Perhaps it'll do him some good to see a real musician in concert.

Kevin E. Smith, Age 29
Editor, *The Horizon,* Indiana University Southeast
Jeffersonville, Indiana
September 30, 2002

This story first appeared in a slightly different format in Kevin E. Smith's column in *The Horizon* on 9/30/02.

Reprinted with permission.

An Artist's Tale

Sometimes I am amazed at the coincidences that happen in life. It all started a few months ago when I was bored and decided to paint a picture of John Lennon. Towards the end of September 2002, I entered the painting into the local fair's art competition (along with numerous other pieces). I got a call a few days later from a teenage guy named Roger asking to buy my painting. I said yes, and we talked for a while. Half an hour later, he called back to invite me to the Paul McCartney concert in Atlantic City that coming Saturday, September 28...free of charge! Of course, I said yes.

It just all seems so unreal to me. I mean, I've gotten things from Yoko, and I've seen Julian in concert, but it still seems like the Beatles never really happened. I don't know how to explain it. I guess it's because I wasn't alive when the Beatles were together, so Paul is just a voice on a CD, or a picture in a book. It was hard for me to grasp the fact that I would be seeing him perform.

My new friend, his parents, and I all had a great time in Atlantic City...walking the boardwalk, seeing the sights. The beach was beautiful! Wonderful weather, as well. Roger paid $150 each for his tickets, and they were the cheap seats! He said that Paul hadn't been in Atlantic City since the Beatles played there. Our seats were pretty far back, but the center was fairly small, so it wasn't too bad.

The 'opening act' before Paul's performance had a bunch of Mozart-looking people and what looked like circus performers. It was all right (especially the woman who folded herself into that small box...now that was cool!), but really strange...and too long. But, when the silhouette of Paul's guitar appeared on the white screen, the crowd went WILD!

The concert was (almost) musically perfect! I loved the tributes...especially the one to John. People applauded for what seemed like a few minutes after the George and John tributes. They were the most touching songs, as far as I'm concerned. Honestly – you'd literally have to be brain-dead not to enjoy this show. Even if you were hearing-impaired, the visual display was out of this world, and would've kept you entertained easily. It was strange being practically the youngest ones in the crowd, though. People kept asking us where our parents were (keep in mind...we're 18 – we didn't need to have our parents with us!) At one point, I went out to a pay phone and let most of *Freedom* record on my mom's cell phone. I know she would've loved to have been there to see "her" Paul.

Of course, no one wanted the concert to end, and Paul came out for a few encores. It was wonderful! What an amazing experience!

Kristin Turberville, Age 18
Bloomsburg, Pennsylvania

Some of my Beatles artwork appears on the next three pages. The first one, the painting of John, is the one that got me a free ticket to Paul McCartney's concert.

A Young Bespectacled John Lennon

This painting has a very special place in my heart. Not only is it my first painting to have been sold, but it also is the reason that I got to go to a Paul McCartney concert. Anyway, I took a picture of an early John in the recording studio and altered it on Adobe Photoshop to look like a stamp, or print. I then drew onto a canvas and painted it different colors. It only took a few hours to complete (because it's rather small), so it would be easy to duplicate if need be. It's unique in its own little way.

(A Young Bespectacled John Lennon: 2002: Oil on Canvas Board: 8x10)

Kristin Turberville, Age 18
Bloomsburg, Pennsylvania

http://www.angelfire.com/art2/kristinturberville/artwork3.html

Lennon Ceiling Tile

As a high school senior, I was permitted to paint one of the ceiling tiles in the art room. I had wanted to create my own ever since I was a freshman sitting in Humanities class, staring at each of the different painted squares in the ceiling. To my luck, no one had done a Lennon or Beatles tile, so (of course) I made a Lennon one. This was my first attempt at painting realistically.

To make mine a little different from the other tiles, I used only blue and white tempera paints. The face and hand are purposely more realistic than the body and guitar. I did this to draw attention to the face. I also did the lettering in stencils (which are a pain!)

I hope my ceiling tile brings happiness to another bored Humanities student some day.

Awards/Recognitions: This tile will forever be displayed in Central Columbia High School, Bloomsburg, PA.
(*Lennon Ceiling Tile*: 2001: Tempera on Fiberglass Tile: 24x24)

Kristin Turberville, Age 17
Bloomsburg, Pennsylvania

Imagine

 This drawing was inspired by the back cover of John Lennon's early solo album, *Imagine*. A cousin visited my house and challenged me to a drawing contest. He eventually gave up, and I finished the drawing a few days later. This gave me an opportunity to practice bone structure and human profiles. I chose not to draw the background scene because I wanted the drawing to focus on John. He appears to be lying down, looking up into the sky – at peace.

Awards/Recognitions: This drawing won an Honorable Mention ribbon at the 2000 Bloomsburg, PA Fair. This drawing also received a ribbon for participation in the 16 & under category for the 2000 Chicago Beatlefest Art Contest. This drawing is displayed on Bagism's Exhibit 11 on the Art & Poetry page.
(*Imagine*: 1999: Pencil on Paper: 8x10)

Kristin Turberville, Age 16
Bloomsburg, Pennsylvania

http://www.angelfire.com/art2/kristinturberville/artwork3.html

Hey Jude

Fishing by the lake of the invisible,
hooking picture framed visions,
swimming in spaces of dreams:
Twisted Love and Flowers turn into Music.

Drinking cups of Indian music
with spiritual vision biscuits,
walking the tightropes of Art and Love
juggling crisp, green apples.

"You say you want a revolution"
as guitars weep,
sweeping waters down gutters.

A world spins around,
nervously unfolding
and plotting its atlas
towards the moon.

Cracked off frosty shadows,
rubbed window panes,
clear tunnels of sleep,
subways to imagination billboards.

A. J. P. Molloy

Dark Horse

Mystical passion
turning suns inside out,
facing inverted reality,
whispering space and time
of Past, Present and Future.

Remembering all those years
sealed in smiles of the past.
Laughing, coughing:
A spider in the heart
tickling and splitting happiness
into fragments of mirrors.

An orange shirt and white suit,
sing for the starved,
dig up Light and Love:
The Art of Dying.

A driving Rock and Roll beat
burns his voice,
screeched around corners
hiding from the webs of fame,
wanting his own chequered flag.

A. J. P. Molloy

Acting Naturally

Fingers smoulder
in burning, silver circles:
Flashing rings glaze
under theatrical leaves,
blowing restlessly over
shadows of movie films.

Clicking photographs,
melted negatives
hum the sweet, fresh laughter
in songs of youth:
"You're Sixteen."

Dissolving under guitars
and crashing drums,
he belts a thousand hammers,
blazing and bouncing
basketball suns
thump on fire, crusted planets.

He stops to smell blood, curled fabric:
the thrilled red stars
twisting and laughing
on green wired fuses
of ladders to springtime.

A. J. P. Molloy

Starting Over

Sky people
lock it in the cupboard,
watch shadows rot
plastic time images.

They stroll in Central Park
hand in hand. Two Flowers
living a reality together,
breathing a dream:
Summer 1980.

Dakota Days,
folding nappies, baking loaves of bread,
spinning laughter records:
The black vinyl discs of the Heart.

Rock and roll again:
He shakes a bottle of comeback champagne,
bubbling family and happiness messages.

A pudgy face and vacant stare.
Stranger firing from shadows,
clutching a 'Double Fantasy' LP
smashes the silence.

Fans at the Dakota
bring single flowers,
pin little love notes to the wall,
sing in union,
hold up pictures beside
flickering flames in hands cupped together.

Mathew Street, Cavern Club:
"Four Lads who shook the world."

Dusk spilling grey, shadowy blood
dripping over New York,
trapping the world
in scattered confusion.
Cold cotton ball clouds
falling gently
and stretching back to Liverpool.

A. J. P. Molloy

Andrew Molloy, Age 33
Sydney, Australia

The poems by A. J. P. Molloy were previously published at
http://www.beatles.net/ a part of
http://www.AustralianMedia.com/
Reprinted with permission.

So Much Younger Than Today: Memories Of My Hometown Heroes

I am a lad from Liverpool who now lives in the States. Being from the same city as the Fab Four meant that we grew up with them whether we liked it or not.

I didn't know or meet the Beatles, but we all felt as though we did. They were *ours*. Our heroes, our friends, part of our family. When the Beatles conquered the States in 1964, it wasn't just their triumph, it was *our* triumph. I remember that the *Liverpool Echo* ran a special newspaper celebrating that first American tour. I still recall the BBC interrupting their Saturday afternoon sports show, Grandstand, to show scenes at the London airport of the lads returning home to crowds of screaming girls, after just having left a hysterical America behind in their wake. A leading British sports commentator, David Coleman, was sent to the airport to interview the Beatles after they touched down. I clearly remember him asking the lads who their favourite soccer team was. John, Paul and George all answered "Liverpool," while Ringo, for a laugh, said the London team, "Arsenal!"

Many of my earliest Beatle memories pre-date their first American tour. I can recall going on holiday with my Auntie Irene and my family in August 1963 to Rhyl in North Wales. Irene was in her late teens/early twenties and she spoke constantly of going dancing in the Cavern Club and, of course, she raved about the Beatles. Although I was quite young, I was music-mad already and loved the popular instrumental group, the Shadows. My Auntie Irene would wind me up by saying that the Beatles were not only the better group, but they were more popular. I disagreed vehemently! I recall that she came across an issue of *Woman's Own* magazine on that holiday. It had a big article saying that the four lads from Liverpool were now bigger and more popular then the Shads. I was crushed! Of course, the musical magic of the Beatles soon held sway and the following Christmas I received my first long-playing record from Santa, *With the Beatles*. I still own that very copy to this day!

My greatest memory of the early Beatles occurred before they had hits, before they were famous, before my Auntie Irene spoke of them, and long before they conquered America. I was party to a little bit of history when they made their first-ever appearance on British television. I understand it was October 1962 when the Beatles appeared on the local news magazine programme, People & Places, on the regional independent television station, Granada. We would often have this show on in the background while we had our evening tea. Most days they would have singers or groups or performers to break up the items of the local news day. I cannot remember any of the other singers featured – it must have been the magic of the moptops. They, for some reason, stuck in my mind. Their destiny and our history were only months away. They played their first single, *Love Me Do,* and another song that I cannot recall. They were introduced by the host as having just returned from a triumphant trip to Hamburg in Germany. Oh, and John played harmonica!

Little did any of us suspect the effect these four lads would have not only on our lives, but on the entire world. From small acorns...

Ralph Ferrigno, Age 47
Beverly, Massachusetts
(Formerly of Liverpool, England)

When In Sixty-Four

Reflecting on today being February 7, 2003 and a Friday, just as February 7th was in 1964, is having a strange effect on me. I'm finding it hard to focus on anything except the Beatles. Things certainly haven't changed much in 39 years in *that* regard. I can't believe it was 39 years ago today! Has it really been that long? Can that be possible?

I'll never forget the thrill and exhilaration of Friday, February 7, 1964, when we knew they'd soon be arriving at John F. Kennedy International Airport in Queens. The Beatles were all I could think about that day in school. The sense of excitement and anticipation was way beyond anything I'd known at that point. I'd just turned thirteen, the perfect age to completely succumb to this amazing music and these four beautiful men ... particularly Paul. My poor, fragile thirteen-year-old heart never stood a chance against that face and those eyes.

Living in New York City, which was the focal point of much of the Beatle activity in America in February 1964, just added to the frenzy and excitement. I felt so connected to everything that was happening. The Beatles would be landing in Queens, a few miles from where I lived. Earlier that week, the deejays on the radio had started announcing the time in Beatle minutes ("It's now fifteen Beatle minutes past six!") and announcing the temperature outside as "27 Beatle degrees!" All this heightened our anticipation and delight over their impending arrival on Friday afternoon.

In school, those of us who loved the Beatles could barely get through the day because of our exuberance over their arrival. We knew that their plane was due to land in the early afternoon. No one paid attention to anything in class. We speculated about what the Beatles might be doing at any given moment that day. We passed notes to each other about the Beatles during every class. In those days, we fancied ourselves as being adept at passing notes without the teachers seeing. That day, those sheets of paper ripped from our little spiral-bound assignment pads traveled miles due to all the fervent note-passing that went on. All the notes were about the Beatles. What did we write about? All sorts of things. Important things, like what we were going to serve them for dinner if they came to our houses while they were in New York.

One major problem for me, however, was the Bat Mitzvah that Friday evening of a classmate named Janet. How clearly I remember her 39 years later, solely based on her link to that day! Janet had short, curly red hair, wore brown-rimmed glasses, and was one of the smartest kids in the class. She excelled in math and science, the banes of my existence. She was the one who always ruined the curve on tests for the rest of the class. I remember her as if she's sitting next to me now, only because of her direct impact on me that day.

All I wanted to do on February 7, 1964, was race home after school and turn on the radio and listen to my two favorite rock and roll stations, WMCA and "W-A-*Beatles*-C," as WABC-AM had just anointed itself. That had become their station jingle: W-A-*Beatles*-C!! and they'd repeat it continually. I wanted to hear the minute-by-minute reports and the continuous Beatles music on both stations. I wanted to watch the evening news to see the thrilling footage of their actual arrival at the airport. I wanted to think of nothing but the Beatles and just be totally lost and immersed in them.

Instead, that Friday evening, I had to get dressed up and be dragged off to attend Janet's Bat Mitzvah service. I didn't want to go. I just wanted to remain completely immersed in my Beatles rapture, but I had replied many weeks earlier (before I had any idea of the historic day that February 7th was going to be) that I'd attend. One of the other parents was picking us up. I desperately wanted to stay home, but my mother made me go. So, off I went, completely wretched and miserable, feeling that this was all terribly unfair. I didn't like Janet that much, anyway. Certainly not enough to have her interfere with my Beatle bliss.

I sat there in the synagogue, listening to a seemingly endless service. One can imagine how difficult it was to sit there when I was thirteen years old and wanting to concentrate on nothing except the Beatles, rock and roll, and my precious Paul. All I could think about was how much I was missing by not being next to my radio, switching the dial back and forth between WMCA and W-A-*Beatles*-C.

Somehow I made it through that evening. I was free!!! Nothing else would get in the way of my Beatles euphoria. I devoted the rest of the weekend to Beatle activities. My best friend Judy and I spent time cutting up newspapers and *Sixteen* magazine in order to save every last article and photo of the Beatles in our scrapbooks. We listened to the radio and played Beatle records over and over on my portable record player. If we went outdoors, we took our transistor radios and walked around with them so that we wouldn't miss any Beatles music or news. Paul was Judy's favorite too, so several times we argued in earnest over which one of us Paul was going to marry. That entire weekend, all the excitement was building up to the big event: the Beatles' incredible performance on the Ed Sullivan Show Sunday night.

It's so strange, but 39 years later, the only girls I remember from my seventh grade class – besides the few girls I was very friendly with outside of school – are Janet and another classmate named Jackie, because of their connection to that unforgettable weekend.

Jackie's father worked for CBS Television in New York and he was able to get her into the audience for the February 9th Ed Sullivan Show. The rest of us were so envious! We thought she was the luckiest girl on the planet. Earlier that week, she told everyone in school that she was going to the Ed Sullivan Show and that she was allowed to invite one friend to go. We all begged Jackie to choose us. She chose, of course ... Janet. It was clear that there was no shortage of ways for Janet to ruin this weekend for me.

Well, here it is, Friday, February 7, 2003 ... 39 years to the day ... and *still* ... the Beatles are all I can think about.

Linda Schultz, Age 52
Newton, Massachusetts
February 7, 2003

The Beatles: A Poem

Lennon and McCartney
created quite a party.
Harrison and Ringo,
they also knew the lingo.

Love is The Word,
they finally heard.
They spread by example,
for within they had ample.

Funny and sincere,
with them, we lost our fear.
Be ourselves, you and me.
And our sorrow, Let It Be.

It's Getting Better
all the time.
Magical Mystery
spinning rhyme.

And when they got older
losing their hair,
the scope of their impact
still can't compare.

John he was snuffed
Imagine….that.
He cried for Help,
by Buddha he sat.

And George he was Something,
   you agree, was he not?
Here Comes the Sun,
   his guitar was hot.

Ringo was solid,
   best drummer we've seen.
you'll catch him aboard
   a Yellow Submarine.

And Paul he was laid
   by the chimney with care.
28 If,
   Uncle Albert was there.

I can't say enough
   'bout this Liverpool group.
Their presence is heartening,
   like a good bowl of soup.

So thank you, Fab Four,
   for the love you did make.
And in the end,
   that love you will take.

As you can tell from my poem, my love for the Beatles is enormous. I firmly believe that for ten years these young men were truly tapping into a beautiful creativity to which no one else has ever come close.

My brothers Patrick, Thomas, and I (we were 6, 5, and 7 respectively) saw the Ed Sullivan program in '64. I still remember it. As children of CIA parents, we moved to Caracas, Venezuela, and I remember my mom taking us to a movie theater in 1965 to watch *Help!* I remember this distinctly, because afterwards we were waiting outside and I had to pee and my mom told me that's what God made bushes for.

Our next tour of duty was in Guatemala and I remember getting *Rubber Soul* and being totally blown away when I heard *Norwegian Wood*. I truly believe this was the first song that separated early Beatles from the later, more sophisticated songs, which I prefer.

My brother, James, who was born in '63, is a huge Beatles fan. Last summer he and I visited Patrick, who lives in Los Cabos, Mexico. We sang many a Beatles song while drinking margaritas by a pool overlooking the Pacific.

I have a twelve-CD player in my car (Patrick's gift to my Dad, and now me) loaded with Beatles. My daughter, Joanie, who is two years and nine months, sings a pretty good *Lucy in the Sky,* though she does say "ribber" instead of river.

Yes, I do believe the Beatles spoke to our souls. Their message of love is desperately needed in a world torn apart by less awakened people who do not realize we are truly one. My poetry tries to reflect this simple truth.

John Sanchez, Age 46
Bowie, Maryland

A Shea Stadium Tale

In 1965, my mother took me to Shea Stadium to see the Beatles. I was only seven years old at the time!

I remember they were wearing those greenish colored double-breasted suits and I was fixated on Ringo Starr. The teenage girls were hysterical – crying, screaming, fainting, you name it. There were huge crowds of girls rushing towards the field, and the police were attempting to force them back up into the stands.

Suddenly, a horde of girls came running down the aisle where our seats were (there must have been fifty of them), and the police met them head-on right where I was sitting. In the ensuing melee, all those girls fell into our seats, crushing me under their weight. The next thing I remember, the cops were pulling me by the arms out from under this mountain of screaming, crying, hysterical girls. They were asking me if I was all right and holding me up above the crowd. I have been a Beatles fan ever since!

Candi Van Wagner, Age 45
Doylestown, Pennsylvania

Thoughts On John Lennon

John Lennon was the coolest guy who ever lived.

"Cool" is such a subjective term. The same was always said of James Dean and Marlon Brando in the 1950s. This reputation was bestowed on them because they had "attitude." But "cool" and "attitude" are not necessarily the same thing. What John Lennon had came from some other place besides an attitude, which he also did happen to have. If John had an attitude, it's completely understandable. His father left him when he was a very young child. His mother left him to be raised by his aunt and then was tragically killed by a drunk driver when she and John had just begun to renew their relationship. John was just a teenager, completely unprepared for her death. Yes, he did have an attitude, and justifiably so, but it was only part of what made John Lennon the coolest guy to ever live.

I don't remember being particularly focused on him individually the first time I saw him on TV on that fateful Sunday night in February of 1964. The only thing that really stood out about him that night was the caption under his face that said, "Sorry girls, he's married." The whole band was cool. Ringo Starr just looked like the happiest drummer ever. Paul McCartney was also grinning from ear to ear and sang with such energy. George Harrison concentrated on his guitar playing and occasionally broke out in a broad smile. John Lennon just played his guitar and sang. Effortlessly. John always looked the most natural at what he did. He always made it look easy.

Within six months, the Beatles' first film was released. This would be the time that John would come into his own as the epitome of cool for me. I may never actually figure out why I was so impressed by John's performance of *If I Fell*...but what a performance!! The way he carries himself in *A Hard Day's Night* is astounding. For starters, look at the way John launches into this song. He casually strums his guitar, and sings as if he were born doing it.

John's sense of humor was no less than legendary. In one of the opening scenes in *A Hard Day's Night*, the conflict with the older, stuffy, "establishment" businessman on the train sets the pace, and is quite telling of John's razor-sharp wit. When the clearly irritated, much-too-proper-for-the-Beatles'-liking businessman insists on closing the window and turning off the lads' radio, they deal with him in different ways. George makes a sour face at him. Paul gives him a speech, and Ringo loudly protests when the man grabs his radio and switches it off. John merely bats his eyes at the man and then a moment later just leans in close to him and says, "Give us a kiss!" Watch the expression on John's face throughout this whole scene. The other three Beatles are indignant, wide-eyed, and amazed at this man's attitude. John just takes on this "enemy" full force, with nothing more than an attitude of his own. He never gives the poor man an inch and then zeroes in on him for the kill. He blankly stares at the man as if he were a statue. Yes, John was cool.

To me, "cool" is individuality and being unique. It's also being ground-breaking. John, of course, was both. As a child, I remember not understanding certain dialogue in the first two Beatles films. I always thought it was the British dialect or expressions. Now I know it was just John. He didn't exactly give stock answers when asked a question. When the others find an old man in their hotel closet, clad in only his underwear, John's response is an unrattled "There you go!" When Victor Spinetti's fussy director character comes out to rave at them, John responds with a question of his own, a very calm "How do you turn into black and white, the situation somewhat?" I also like the scene in the corridor with the woman who insists John looks just like *"him."* John is ready for this sparring session the moment she stops him. That's what I love about his character in this film. He always seems to know what's about to be asked, and he's always at the ready with an answer you will be thinking about for a long time...thirty-nine years, as of this writing! When he tries to sneak off with a chorus girl after a stage rehearsal, he's asked, "Where are you going?" His answer, though not as unusual, but just as funny, is, "She's going to show me her stamp collection!" He then oinks at the figure of authority, and points his finger at him. For me, one of the most enjoyable parts of *A Hard Day's Night* is John's scene playing with toy boats and submarines in the bubble bath. It was complete improvisation. He was the Robin Williams or Jonathan Winters of his time. They shot several minutes of him "winging it" in his exaggerated German accent, and wonderful, childlike play. I truly wish I could see the outtakes of this scene. They must be wonderful to behold.

Then there is *Help!* The group's second film found them doing more and traveling the world. By now they'd found marijuana. The Beatles, and particularly John, always looked like they had a secret they weren't telling anyone else. In several of the early filmed song performances, he would smile as if he were thinking, "If you only knew!" By the making of the second film, they really did have a secret they didn't dare tell. The group in later years spoke of ruining take after take because of stoned laughter and lost concentration on their lines. John's quote was, "By the time we made *Help!,* we were smoking marijuana for breakfast." Apparently the same thing happened during lunchtimes because it's been said that not a lot was accomplished after the lunch hours during shooting of the film.

But what developed during this time was the factor of real secrets, for which most of the world was not quite ready. John's attitude was now a little more downbeat and grim. In later years he described this as his "fat Elvis period" and said he wasn't particularly happy during this time. The coolness prevailed, though. He still had the unique approach to answering a question. "Hey, Beatle, you shall have fun, eh?"

asked the evil Clang. John's answer was, "No, thanks, I'm rhythm guitar and mouth organ." Watch his face; he's so casual and cool in this moment. It comes off as an inside joke while it also has that vicious Lennon edge to it. The Beatles were being pushed and pulled in so many directions by this point in time that it's really no wonder they became so fond of shutting out the noise and the fast pace by being stoned all the time. The viciousness is still there in John's simple statements to other figures of authority. "You've failed, scientist!" he says again to Victor Spinetti. To the Scotland Yard policeman he asks, "How's the Great Train Robbery going?"

The music from *Help!* is just as wonderful as that of their previous film. The one song here that John seems to be remembered for is *You've Got to Hide Your Love Away*. Could anyone ever look more relaxed and more cool than John, as he's leaning back, and just singing and playing his acoustic guitar in this performance? The song before it, *You're Gonna Lose That Girl,* is just as effective with its rich colors and bright lights and shadows of the smoky studio, as John once again plays and sings in such an apparently effortless fashion. His musical performances in these two films still amaze me to this day, after all these years.

Now, it could be argued that many of these examples of "cool" were scripted. True. But John's attitude and personality were not. Neither were the things he said in his daily life. John was never afraid to take a stand, something that would become much more obvious in later years. He often argued with the Beatles' manager, Brian Epstein, over taking a public stance on the war in Vietnam. John and his bandmates wanted to speak out about it during the early days of their popularity, but Brian always insisted that the Beatles not enter into the controversy. Eventually, there was no stopping John's opinions. Epstein was the proverbial boy with his finger in the dike, and John's opinions would eventually come flooding out.

Those opinions became the controversy itself when his observation that the Beatles were more popular than Jesus Christ was taken completely out of context. It was quite a foolish and quick-to-judge segment of America that came down on the entire group so harshly for something that John had said rather off-the-cuff. Besides all that, it appeared to be the truth. Kids were begging their parents to let them go to the concerts. Kids covered their bedroom walls with Beatles pictures. They played their records and bought the magazines and other Beatle merchandise in record numbers. Kids showed no such enthusiasm for the church or any other institution of the time.

John made his statement out of frustration as much as anything. By this time, he was rather weary of the game as it was. He'd lived in the fishbowl of celebrity for a long time and was in need of a rest when this happened. At Brian's insistence, John finally made a public apology for something he'd never really even done in the first place. At this point in time, the Beatles were such a huge machine that couldn't be stopped, but the press wanted an "I'm sorry." Eventually John had to come up with it or the machine would break down, and horribly so. I think it's one of the very few things he did that was not cool. He compromised his principles just to keep a peace that he would eventually very publicly seek out and encourage from the rest of the world. He later said that he was sorry he apologized. I think people are often required to do certain things they truly don't want to do. Like a defense attorney defending an obviously guilty client, John played their game just to move forward. I still admire him for sacrificing his own principles for the greater good of the group, though. Now *that* was pretty cool!

Time went on and things began to change. The influence of the substances and a new musical hero, Bob Dylan, had an effect on all of the Beatles, and especially on John. The songs evolved from the love songs and simplicity of the earlier days and simple rock and roll to something quite different. *I'm a Loser* is really a brave statement to make, if you really think about it! But, as John admitted in later years, that was how he felt at the time. The excitement and freshness of his group had faded for John as they found success. By the time of the second film and the *Beatles For Sale* album, the bloom was long off the rose. It's no wonder he was so introspective at the time; what was there left to conquer?

Anything is fun when it's new and fresh. For John, rock and roll was neither fun nor fresh by this time. Neither was the marijuana. A search for "something new and different" would send them all in different directions in future months. For John, LSD was one of these directions and a significant one for a while. More secrets to keep from the rest of the world. Then the "answers" and "awareness" they were in search of seemed to be closer. Putting an end to the touring would at least let them have a little more time for the "search."

With this new approach, the Beatles decided to just send filmed segments of their new songs to TV shows rather than appear on the shows in person. Why bother going? To promote an album so people would buy it? They'd done that. Have a hit record and let it sail up the charts to number one? They'd done it dozens of times by now. What they did, as George Harrison says in the *Anthology* video, was invent what later became MTV and music videos, as they are now commonly known. I remember feeling slightly cheated when the group stopped showing up to perform live on Ed Sullivan's stage. But when Ed showed a filmed performance by the Beatles, they were *still* cool!

I do remember longing for more, but soon the films of *Hey Jude* and *Revolution* made up for all of the longing to see them again. Today's generation of fans takes for granted that they can go over to the TV, fire up the VCR and watch the Beatles perform these songs in the *Anthology* video series. Back then, we saw them do *Revolution* on a Sunday night on the Smothers Brothers Show, and then the following Sunday we saw Paul at his piano as the others backed him on *Hey Jude*. Then it was years before I saw these clips again. It staggers the mind to think that John died a couple of years before VCRs became commonplace in households around the world. But back then, waiting for them to turn up on a TV program was the *only* way we were able to see them. They were always worth waiting for. Like the annual showing of *The Wizard of Oz,* also usually a Sunday event that I'd look forward to...it was something that drew us to the television before the program even started. We were ready to see the magic for this brief time.

With the Beatles, it always got briefer. In the early days it was a couple of different segments and five or six songs per show. Later, though, it was the one song only, and it was a very controlled filmed performance. Gone were the smiles on their faces in reaction to the screaming audience members. To this fan, though, they were just too cool to smile by now, anyway. They all had attitude and they had given all that they were going to give to live audiences. To me, they were "locked away" somewhere and I simply had to wait for them to come back with a new song to promote sometime in the future.

Even the movies had been fleeting. The films were ninety-plus minutes, of course, but a couple of years later they were long gone from the theaters and remained only as happy memories for their fans. Even in 1976 or so, I remember making a point of getting home early on a Saturday night because a local channel was showing *A Hard Day's Night*. Now I can just go downstairs and pop all of their songs and all of their films and performances in the VCR. The music and movies still hold fascination today, but back then when we couldn't control when we saw or heard them, they were even more fascinating. We could see them only when they appeared on TV, and never at any other time. Hard to believe, in this day of VCRs and DVD players. But they were always worth waiting for...because they were still cool. *Rubber Soul* and *Revolver* brought new sounds to the world, but they were still the same four guys and that's all I cared about. I would go to the library and take out these records, along with the earlier ones. *Revolver* featured really ground-breaking music. The Indian sounds, and John's songs in particular, were so different than anything else we were hearing at the time. Listen to a few songs from the other groups of 1966 and then listen to *Tomorrow Never Knows*. You'll see just how different and cool they were.

Along with the changes within the Beatles came the changes in John. They were hand-in-hand and it's hard to say which was cause and effect. When the touring ended, he had no idea of just what he should do with himself. First he went to Germany and then to Spain, to act in a film called *How I Won the War* for Richard Lester, the man who had directed the Beatles films. John felt a real need to do something with his time and break new ground artistically. He'd already published two books and been in the world's most successful musical group. Acting was at least something new and different. Neil Aspinall, the Beatles' faithful roadie, accompanied him. After a while, John found himself to be lonely and bored and invited Ringo to come and visit him.

One very significant thing happened there, though. John wrote possibly the coolest song ever, *Strawberry Fields Forever*. It was a fond memory for John, who, as a child, had known a real place with that name, but it was much more than that. It was introspective and it was pleading for something different, something unidentifiable. Strawberry Fields was a special place and special state of mind, perhaps. The writing of the song, the recording of the song and eventually the actual sound and feel of the ground-breaking tune is what solidifies John as the coolest songwriter/ performer ever for me. I have strong memories of hearing *Strawberry Fields Forever* as a kid. I have one really vivid memory of hearing it at an outdoor skating rink one winter.

The part that fades out and then fades back in at the end – I can remember that echoing outside over the loudspeakers in the park surrounding the ice rink. I was about eleven or twelve years old, and I knew it was different than other songs I'd heard on the radio. It's exciting to think about now because the memory of it is still so strong. Later on, I also remember going to the house of a friend who had a really good stereo and he owned the album. He was the one who told me about "I buried Paul." He played the end of the 33-1/3 record at 45 speed, and it seemed clear to me that John really had said that!

Two days after John returned from Spain, an event occurred that would truly change his life forever. The thing he'd really and truly been searching for came into his life when John met Yoko Ono, and the rest, as they say, was history. When he first heard about "this new artist" and followed his instincts by going to see "something different, a happening," he found something he truly appreciated and admired. He climbed up a ladder at the exhibition, leaned over and used a magnifying glass to read the small word printed on the piece. The word was "Yes." It was positive and he was impressed.

It was the genesis for one of the greatest love stories and also one of the oddest. John had found someone who was much more important than his bandmates or pop music in general. Unfortunately for Cynthia Lennon, John's wife at the time, Yoko would soon become more of a priority to John than the mother of his only child. Yoko corresponded with John while the Beatles and their wives or girlfriends went off to India to study with the Maharishi Mahesh Yogi. After they were all back, and Cynthia was away for a night, the romance of John and Yoko began when the two spent an entire night making a recording and then made love as the sun rose after the all-night session. Afterwards John told her they would be together forever.

It wasn't long before the press had nothing short of the proverbial "field day" with John and Yoko. She was "horrible," she was a "dragon lady," she was this, and she was that. Beatle fans were up in arms! How could he leave Cynthia? Unflattering photos of John and Yoko seemed to fuel the fire. I always thought, if he loved her, then what was everyone's problem?

I was probably just about thirteen years old when I first became aware of Yoko. I would be about thirty-five or so when I would finally understand why John was so attracted to this woman. Around 1989, I went to see an exhibit of John's art here in my hometown and Yoko was going to be there on the opening night of the exhibit. I showed up hours early, walked in as if I belonged there, and was hoping just to catch a glimpse of the woman John loved for the last few years of his life. I was rather quickly told I did not belong there and was invited to come back when the public was invited in. A few hours later, I did return and saw a white limousine outside the building. Something told me it was hers...and it was. There was now a crowd around the building and they were still not being allowed in. My guess is that there were one hundred to two hundred people waiting to see Yoko, the exhibit, or both.

A side door finally opened and the crowd scrambled towards it. Out stepped Yoko Ono just a few feet away from where I stood. Instantly I knew why John was so attracted to her. She was tiny and she was beautiful. I'd never seen a picture that did her appearance any justice whatsoever. This was my very first thought as I looked at her standing with some very large bodyguards around her. A few girls in the crowd starting singing the refrain of *Give Peace a Chance*. A man stepped out of the crowd and handed her a copy of *John & Yoko's Wedding Album* and asked her if she would autograph it. She politely refused, saying, "I'm sorry, but I won't because it wouldn't be fair to the others." Clearly she was not going to sign anything for anyone else, so she wouldn't sign one for him either.

She began to speak to the crowd and I worried that the girls who were singing would drown her out. They stopped and she finally said in her familiar voice, "Thank you all for coming. I think John would be really proud that you came to see his artwork." That was just about all she had to say and in a moment the men surrounding her cleared a path to the limo and they soon drove off. I'm so glad I saw her, though. I've never seen a decent picture of her to this day that portrays how she really looks. But I got to see her with my own eyes and finally understand why John was so smitten with the woman. While the press and much of the world put them down and made fun of Yoko, John stuck by her. His attitude was, "Let them talk." Few relationships could withstand all the adversity that theirs endured. John always stuck by her. For this alone, John could be considered the coolest guy around.

After John and Yoko became an item publicly, the world was in for yet another shocker. They were releasing a new album together and the cover would feature a photograph of the two of them in the nude. It was only the first of many times that the press and people of the world would ask, "What are they up to *now?*" John would later explain, "We felt like two virgins because we were in love, just met, and we were trying to make something and we thought to show everything. People are always looking at people like me, trying to see some secret: 'What do they do? Do they go to the bathroom? Do they eat?' So we just said, 'Here.' It was insane. People got so upset about it – the fact that two people were naked."

Nobody understood it, nobody liked it and most people just thought that John should "stop all of this stuff" and go back to being the guy that sang *I Want to Hold Your Hand*. But there was no turning back for John. He not only had the world's attention, but it was affecting his band...and he didn't care, either. Instead of "meeting her after work," John brought Yoko straight into the recording sessions and she sat right beside him in the studio. It was something the other Beatles had never done, or even *thought* of doing. John had broken their "unwritten law" about bringing a woman into the recording studio. He wanted nothing less than to be with Yoko twenty-four hours a day. What the other three members of his band thought mattered not one bit to John. By this time, the Beatles were not exactly the same happy little group they had once been. Brian Epstein had died while they were in Bangor, Wales, with the Maharishi. Business problems were beginning to pile up quickly. Bringing Yoko to every Beatle session made an unhappy situation even less happy. The others were resentful. The truth was that John didn't care. He knew the others didn't want her there, but he kept his cool. He kept it right up until the time he got the chance to do something else he really wanted to do. He quit the Beatles. Broke them up. Put an end to them. Told them he "wanted a divorce."

While the world remained unaware of this for many more months, John and Yoko continued to make news of their own. They got married and then decided to have a honeymoon in an Amsterdam hotel. While that would normally not be too strange, the difference was they also invited the press to their honeymoon and had what would come to be known as "A Bed-In for Peace." Half of the press people expected to see the two of them doing something pornographic after the *Two Virgins* debacle. Instead they found the couple doing what they called "a commercial...for peace." John and Yoko sat in their pajamas and let reporters ask whatever questions they wished. On the walls were signs saying, "Peace," "Love," and things like "Bed Peace." They had a rather odd mixture of celebrities with them as well and the group of onlookers helped sing the chorus as John and Yoko recorded *Give Peace a Chance* in their hotel room. The recording was put out as John's first commercial solo single and was a substantial hit. The Plastic Ono Band was born and it would go through various incarnations over the next few years.

The whole point is this. Through all of the adversity, John stuck by the woman he loved and never doubted what he was doing for a single minute. People called them both crazy, especially John. The world wanted him to go back to being 'their' lovable moptop. But doing what *he* wanted to do and defending Yoko was *better* than cool. It was brave. It was honest. He didn't really risk looking foolish, because he honestly didn't care if he did appear that way. John and Yoko did things such as sending acorns to kings and national leaders, asking them to "plant this for peace." Most of those were thrown away. Today, though, the ones that did indeed get planted in 1969 are beautiful, majestic oak trees. They called their life together art. If you look at one of those trees today, it is indeed a beautiful masterpiece. How cool is this? They literally planted seeds for a better future and we can actually appreciate it today. At least we *should.*

John was always a rebel. Whether against the government or institutions like the church, he always had an axe to grind with someone, and he usually didn't have any problem voicing his opinions. Eventually, it would be his politics that would get him in the most serious trouble of his life. When he released the song, *Power to the People*, it provoked an already paranoid Nixon administration to actually have the CIA tap his phones. John was hanging out with radical types, such as Jerry Rubin and Abbie Hoffman, and he had been busted in England for cannabis possession. He was an outlaw. But he was cool. He was cool and the government *knew* the younger generation thought him to be cool. They were worried that he would organize riots and cause civil unrest, so they broke their own laws in order to run surveillance on him. Fortunately, even though some of the radicals with whom he was friendly wanted his participation in such activities, he eventually did see that they were going about changing society in too violent a fashion, and he turned to more grounded causes. He staged a benefit for mental health institutions. He also stood up for people like John Sinclair, who had been given a ten-year prison sentence for possession of two joints. John wrote a song about it and even staged a benefit concert on Sinclair's behalf. Finally, he fell in love with New York, and decided to make it his home permanently.

As more time passed, John and Yoko eventually came to be separated. This began what was known as John's infamous "lost weekend" in Los Angeles. Many drunken nights with singer Harry Nilsson, the Who's drummer Keith Moon, and Ringo made for now legendary stories of "the boys' wild night out" that actually lasted for months.

When John finally returned to New York to appear on stage with Elton John, he saw Yoko backstage, and their love was rekindled. After all the years of recording with the Beatles, followed by his solo albums, John Lennon was now a man without a recording contract, and he couldn't have been happier. Their fondest wish was just to settle down and try to have a baby. Sean was born in 1975 and the Lennons became a happy little New York family.

The music world wondered "what John was up to now" for five years, and what John was up to, was probably what really defined his life as a man and not as a musician. He called himself a "househusband" and spent time caring for his new son while Yoko tended to old business with Apple and their various business interests. His friends would call and ask what he was doing with his time and he would usually say, "Baking bread." John became the father that he himself never had. He also was now the kind of father he hadn't been to Julian, who had been unlucky enough to be born the son of a very busy young Beatle.

This part of John's life raising Sean isn't just cool...it touches the heart. John got as close to Sean as any father could during this very important time in both of their lives.

He did his "domestic period" like millions of mothers had done for years. John always supported feminism after he met Yoko, once she made him understand that women were not meant to be servants and also not meant for most of the roles which society had assigned to them. John stood by her side and preached feminist causes whenever they appeared in public. Now he actually practiced what they had preached by letting his wife "play businessman" with the talent she had for it, while he took care of the domestic chores and the raising of young Sean. The closeness father and son developed was something that sadly would have only a limited amount of time as John was taken from the world just weeks after Sean's fifth, and John's fortieth, birthdays. The way he switched traditional roles with his wife during the time they lived in the Dakota was very different and unique twenty years ago. It was ground-breaking. It was cool. It still is.

It's difficult to sum up John Lennon's life in a few pages. He was a complicated man. He was capable of writing *How Do You Sleep*, yet he really did love Paul McCartney like a brother. He could sing and sometimes scream a song like *Cold Turkey* or *Well Well Well,* but he was also capable of touching the soul much more softly with a song like *Julia, Look at Me,* or *Oh My Love*. John had a reputation for being cynical. He took people on. He always had an opinion and it wasn't always a popular one.

There is one very special thing I like to remember John for besides his music and the five years he spent with Sean. It's a scene in the *Imagine* documentary that Yoko had made after his death. During the time of recording the *Imagine* album, there was an American hippie sort of guy who was hanging out in John and Yoko's garden, and around the outside of their estate in England. It finally came to John's attention and he went out early one morning to speak to him. John had lived with his fans for years, and he ignored them when he could and sometimes talked to them, but probably only when he was in the mood. John went to this particular person, though, and asked the man what he wanted. It was clear that this was a very lost soul who had come to John in search of some "answers" in his life. As the film continues, John explains to the man that he simply has no answers for him...but then says just three words that I personally want to remember John Lennon for: "Are you hungry?" When the obviously unwashed, unfed man answers John with a very meek "Yeah," John says, "Well, let's give him something to eat," and brings him into his house, and sits him down at the dining room table, and they eat together. It's something that always touches me, just as much as he still makes me laugh when I watch his scenes in *A Hard Day's Night*.

John Lennon was the coolest guy ever. If I haven't convinced you by now, then there's really nothing more I could tell you. If you don't think he rocked hard enough, you never heard *Cold Turkey*. If you think he was just too abrasive of a man, you never heard *Bless You*. Listen and appreciate both and everything in between. It's all cool. So was John.

Steve Clausen, Age 48
St. Louis, Missouri

My Life As A Beatle Fan

It all began on August 13, 1963, the day they first played *She Loves You* on the radio in Britain. That's the exact day I was born (in Gainesville, Florida), although chances were that we weren't receiving BBC transmissions via satellite (or any other media) in Gainesville. Ten days later, on August 23, *She Loves You* was released as a single in Britain.

My mother tells me that I was singing, "Yeah, Yeah, Yeah" in the crib. She used to sing passages of Beatles songs throughout my childhood, so songs such as *All My Loving, Things We Said Today, Yesterday, Michelle, Hey Jude,* and *Ob-La-Di, Ob-La-Da* became familiar to me. When I was young, we lived in the UK while my mother was getting her Ph.D. at Cambridge University. Top of the Pops and the Eurovision song contest were popular on the telly at the time.

The rest of the decade was kind of a blur musically. When I was finally old enough to appreciate music, we were living in Charlottesville, Virginia – not exactly your rock and roll hub! I mainly listened to news radio and Top 40 stations and I relied heavily on my parents' record collection for entertainment. That's where I found a mono version of the *Something New* LP; a European EP with *Yesterday* on it; and a *Yellow Submarine* single. We also had the Carpenters' version of *Ticket to Ride.* I recall seeing one of my fifth grade classmates, Robbie Fulks (later of country music fame) on cable access television performing *When I'm 64* and Elton John singing *Lucy in the Sky with Diamonds.* At the time, I was totally unaware that these last three were Beatles songs!

I was in seventh grade when someone in my singing class brought in the *Listen to What the Man Said* single, which we listened to a bunch of times. It was the summer of *Silly Love Songs* in 1976 when a local radio station presented a six-hour program playing all the Beatles songs. In retrospect, they must have only played clips of the songs, but it was the first time I was exposed to their entire career. There was another Indian family in the neighborhood. They had four sons around my age who all were familiar with the Beatles and they'd often play Beatle songs on guitar.

That summer, we moved to southern New Jersey, which was a musical culture shock. The Philadelphia area provided many different types of rock and roll music on the radio, for which I was not prepared. I held my ground and continued to listen to the Beatles. I bought my first copy of the *Magical Mystery Tour* LP after being fascinated by a TV clip of John Lennon singing *Strawberry Fields Forever*. It was during eighth grade that I ordered a book through one of those school book clubs. The book was called *The Beatles Lyrics Illustrated*. When my English teacher announced that the mail had come in, I was ecstatic to know that I soon would have in my hands the words to *all* the Beatles' songs! But when she handed me an unrelated poster instead, I was practically in tears. This was not what I had ordered. She looked again and found the book I'd been waiting for. Upon reading it, I found the lyrics with which I was familiar…and a whole lot more with which I was *not!* I knew there was work to be done.

My collecting was to be put off for a year, however, as we went to live with my grandparents in India for the 1977-78 school year. I put whatever songs I had, including *Magical Mystery Tour* and other songs from my parents' records, onto a cassette and carried this and my lyrics book with me to India. When I returned to the US as a high school sophomore, I started collecting again. I found a scratchy copy of *Let It Be* in a department store and *Yesterday and Today* in K-mart for $4. I tried to watch *Let It Be* on Cinemax, but I got no picture, so I listened to the entire thing from the TV. I saw the *Beatlemania* show in Philadelphia with one of my neighbors.

By the summer of 1980, I had it all, ending with *Beatles VI* and the two rarities collections that had come out that year. I felt both excited that my collection was complete and disappointed knowing that I wouldn't have the thrill of ever hearing a new Beatles song again. I had now heard all the songs I had lyrics to, except for a few songs that the Beatles had given to other artists. Then I found an LP that had those songs. One of my friends bought me a replacement for my lyrics book, which, by now, was falling apart.

That year brought an abrupt end to everyone's hopes of there ever being a Beatles reunion with the passing of John Lennon. I happened to be sick in bed the day I heard that news. My parents bought me the *Starting Over* single and I bought *Double Fantasy*.

The 1990s began for me with a trip to England to tour London and Liverpool and attend Paul McCartney's concert in Birmingham. What an experience! We attended a New Year's Eve party in Studio Two of Abbey Road, where many of the Beatles' songs were recorded. A Beatles cover band performed in the studio. I saw places in Liverpool from Beatles folklore, including Penny Lane, Strawberry Fields, the Cavern and the Casbah. I saw Paul McCartney perform live for the first time ever. His concert was amazing, despite what I considered to be a rather sedate crowd.

In December of 1991, I was able to attend three George Harrison concerts in Tokyo featuring Eric Clapton and his band. George sounded absolutely incredible. The trip included a concert by a Japanese tribute band called the Parrots at Tokyo's "Cavern Club."

1993 was a very sad year for me as my mother took a turn for the worse in the later stages of cancer. She traveled to England with me, and we made our final visit to Cambridge University.

I got to see Paul perform again, this time at Veterans Stadium in Philadelphia, on June 13, 1993. I won VIP tickets to have a vegetarian dinner, attend the sound check and watch the show from the sound booth. I wrote a birthday card to Paul expressing the sadness I felt over losing my mother to cancer and told him how much she and I loved his music.

In July 1993, we went to deliver my mother's ashes to the Ganges River in Hardwar, Uttar Pradesh, India. After the service by the river, we drove to Rishikesh. Dipping my feet in the river in such a peaceful and serene setting was quite therapeutic, and besides helping me to heal, it also helped me to understand the rationale for the Beatles coming there seeking solace many years earlier.

In 1994, I learned about a special trip to England to retrace the steps of the Beatles in the *Magical Mystery Tour* movie. This sounded quite exciting! That August, around 35 of us congregated in London and boarded a bus for the South of England. The Liverpudlian tour guide tried to keep it a mystery, but the agenda had already been written up in the local newspapers. We stopped in several coastal areas that were part of the original *Magical Mystery Tour* film. The trip concluded in Liverpool in time for the Annual Merseyside Beatles Convention. Cynthia Lennon was one of the convention guests and was treated like royalty. On the last day, we watched the *Magical Mystery Tour* film on video and saw all the places we'd just been.

In August of 1998, I once again toured the Beatles' England. The trip was called the Magical Mystery Tour. We went to Henley-on-Thames where we saw the exterior of George Harrison's estate, Friar Park. The tour guide led us to many London Beatles sites, including Marylebone Station, where the opening scene to *A Hard Day's Night* was filmed. Three of us reenacted this sequence. As "George," I got to run down the street, trip and fall three times – oh, joy! – so that all my tourmates could have a chance to snap pictures.

The next day, we went inside Abbey Road Studio Two, where we recorded *Hey Jude* with a Brazilian tribute band. A BBC-1 TV crew was on hand to document this. Later that evening, back at the hotel, we all crammed into a tiny room to listen to the Beatles' former chauffeur, Alf Bicknell, tell hilarious stories about his days working for the Beatles. The next day we watched the film of ourselves at Abbey Road Studios on British television. We went to a taping of a TV show guest-starring Julian Lennon.

In Liverpool, we toured Paul's childhood home. Seeing the house was great, but there wasn't enough time to listen to all the music and recorded speeches on the handset they gave us to use while walking around the house. The downstairs consisted of a front parlour (living room), a back parlour (dining room) and a kitchen with back door access to a fenced garden. Mike McCartney's family photographs were on the walls of the house. There was a picture of Paul's dad, Jim, looking quite like Paul. There were sad stories recorded about Paul's mom, Mary McCartney, and her last days at the hospital. Upstairs were Paul's and Mike's rooms. They let you sit on the bed in Paul's room to take it all in. It was pretty amazing to actually sit in the front parlour while listening to music that was probably written there.

That night we went to the Liverpool Institute of Performing Arts (LIPA) to hear some more Beatles cover bands. The next day was a walking tour of Liverpool. We saw the hospital where John was born, his art college, and the school that Paul and George had attended. We spent some time in the Anglican Cathedral where, long ago, Paul had been rejected in his bid to be a choir boy. We saw interesting sites (including the park where John's parents met), and the exteriors of the childhood homes of John, George and Ringo. We saw the exterior of Brian Epstein's home, the church where John met Paul, Eleanor Rigby's tombstone, Strawberry Fields and Penny Lane. We saw The

Beatles Story, a museum exhibit chronicling the lives and extraordinary careers of the Beatles.

Our entire group went to the actual Strawberry Fields for a garden party on Sunday afternoon. The event was a benefit concert featuring several tribute bands. We ate strawberry scones and drank strawberry tea. Julia Baird (John Lennon's half-sister) was there signing autographs. I took a break from all this and went over to take pictures in front of John's house on Menlove Avenue – a hop, skip and a jump from Strawberry Fields. The last band of the day, a Japanese tribute band called Wishing, closed the garden party with *Strawberry Fields Forever* – a nice ending to a nice, sunny day!

On the bus back to the hotel, there was an *a capella* group from Italy singing their own Manhattan Transfer style arrangements of Beatles songs. They didn't know the words to *You Won't See Me*, so I filled in on lead for them on that song. It was enjoyable to hear their harmonies singing, "You-a-won't-a-see me." They gave me a hearty "Bravo!" when I finished.

The next day, several of us went to catch the ferry 'cross the Mersey at the Albert Dock. Later, back at the hotel, several bands were performing a concert of all the Beatles albums. Each album was performed in its entirety by a different band. Later we saw Johnny Gentle, who toured with the Beatles early on, and even co-wrote a song with John Lennon which he played for us, twice. Following him was John's half-sister, Julia Baird, who discussed her family projects in India and life growing up with John. Alan Parsons talked about his days at Abbey Road. Downstairs in the nightclub, the Merseybeats (contemporaries of the Beatles) performed. On the last day, I headed down to the Rutles "press conference" featuring Neil Innes and John Halsey, who were quite entertaining. Afterwards, we went to see the Rutles play at the Cavern.

On October 9, 1998, I went to New York's Central Park where Yoko Ono was planting a tree in Strawberry Fields for John Lennon. Lots of people had gathered to view the event. I stood with the crowd up on the rock with the plaque that lists all the countries. From there, you could gaze down through the little valley where seats, a podium, the English Oak tree and several camera crews were set up. It was kind of hard to see past an obstructing tree. It was a multi-cultural crowd. A guitarist started a sing-along with *All You Need is Love.*

Around noon, Yoko and her entourage paraded down from the Dakota. I seized the opportunity to get a little closer to the ceremony while people were looking at Yoko. She took her seat next to several Liverpool and New York high-profile types. The New York City Parks Commissioner and a representative from the mayor's office spoke. Sheila Johnston from The Beatles Story and the Lord Mayor of Liverpool each discussed Lennon's life. The Lord Mayor presented Yoko with the 'Freedom of the City of Liverpool' scroll. Yoko spoke about how well Strawberry Fields was preserved. She and the Lord Mayor each took the shovel and placed a little dirt on the English Oak tree. Yoko went back home. I showed the Lord Mayor my 'Friend of Strawberry Fields' T-shirt that I got at the 'real' Strawberry Fields. I watched the gardeners cover the unlabeled tree with dirt and wood chips and add a fence. I hung around the mosaic while people lit candles and joined in sing-alongs before it started to rain.

On October 20, I found myself in line in New York City once again – this time to meet Ringo Starr in person. I had picked up his *Storytellers* CD before getting in line at Tower Records on Broadway. When I made it to the front of the line, Ringo signed two of my CDs. I told him what an amazing show his recent concert at the Bottom Line was. He thanked me and gave me a left-handed handshake. He was very friendly – full of smiles.

I heard that Ringo was going on tour again and tickets would be available in Atlantic City. I made it to the casino just before tickets went on sale. There was no line and I got a ticket for front and center. The show was incredible – getting to see Ringo perform so close without having to stand.

At Beatlefest in 2001, Paul Saltzman shared his stories of the Beatles in Rishikesh. I had received a copy of his book for Christmas. I explored Saltzman's "Beatles in Rishikesh" exhibit room where he had several photos on display. These had only been shown in Toronto prior to this.

During Beatlefest, we performed *Dehradune*, a song from a Beatles' session in India. It went over well, even though no one was familiar with it. I thought it was appropriate as I had just returned from India the week before. Rishikesh, which is in the same state as Dehradune (Uttar Pradesh, India), was already represented by Paul Saltzman, who shared his slides from India – quite informative.

Although I missed Paul's autograph session in June 2001 in New York, I acquired my very first signature of Paul's through the mail on his *Blackbird Singing* book. The end of November 2001 brought the passing of my hero, George Harrison, as he succumbed to cancer.

2002 began with a new job and my wedding. Our honeymoon began Friday, April 5, 2002 in Las Vegas. The following night we attended Paul McCartney's concert. Our seats were second level, far from the stage. The show started with circus performers and acrobatics; not your usual opening act! Paul came out and the band played several Beatles' and Wings' songs before launching into new material. An acoustic set featured Paul switching back and forth from piano to guitar. Paul did a moving version of *Here Today* for John and an even more moving *Something* arranged for ukulele in honor of George. Hearing *My Love* was probably the most touching part of the show for me.

Beatles songs closed the show. I would see Paul McCartney two more times – in Philadelphia and in New York City – that month.

I turned forty on August 13, 2003, exactly forty years to the day that *She Loves You* had its debut on British radio. Ten days later, on August 23, I went to my company picnic. The theme was the 1960s and a Beatles cover band played at the park. Their opening song happened to be *She Loves You*. It was exactly forty years to the day since its original British release. The band was unaware that this was so, but it makes a fitting end to this narrative.

Vineet (Vinny) Kochhar, Age 40
Maple Shade, New Jersey

Welcome To The Land of Fab

I am involved with a Beatles store in Liverpool called, "From Me To You." The mall is on the site of the original Cavern Club and we receive guests from around the world making their pilgrimage to "Beatle Wonderland."

I reveal to our visitors that although they are standing on the site of the original club and possibly even the site of the stage, the Beatles did not have their first paid gig there. Their first official paid engagement took place in a small village over the Mersey River called Port Sunlight Village on Saturday, 18th August 1962. I was six years old at the time and lived just around the corner...I still do! It was the village horticultural show (gala) and admission was six shillings (about 30p). Although Ringo had stood in on one or two occasions at the Cavern, this was the first official John, Paul, George and Ringo performance. I often take our guests from the shop over to the hall where this gig took place.

My dad, Frank, was one of the four doormen that day. He remembers taking tickets from the queue at the front and selling them to the people at the back! I remember that my dad said at the time that the Beatles "were too loud and not very good."

Steve Barnes, Age 47

From Me To You Beatlestore and Information Centre
Cavern Walks Shopping Mall, Mathew Street
Liverpool L2 6RE, England

www.beatles64.co.uk

liverpoolaccent@yahoo.co.uk (e-mail)

She's Leaving Home

There is a nice story about the day a young girl, just twenty-one years old, entered our store and explained that she had just walked and hitchhiked her way from Russia to Liverpool. She stated her mission: to meet Paul McCartney in person...as simple as that! "Oh, yeah!" I scoffed. "Another one, and as for walking from Russia...as IF!!"

Well, after she showed me photos of herself standing next to just about every road sign between Moscow and Liverpool, I began to take her seriously. It turned out that she had traveled from the Urals, a distance of about 5,000 miles. She spent three days on a train to Moscow and then made her way to Liverpool. We looked after her as best we could and then she disappeared.

The next time I saw her was in *The Sunday Times* newspaper! There was a photograph of her sitting on a wall and holding a piece of cardboard on which she had written: "I've walked from Russia. Can I come in?" The photo was taken outside the venue of Sir Paul's poetry reading at Hay-on-Wye. Someone from MPL spotted her and placed her in the front row. Paul was informed of it and the next thing she knew, she was on stage speaking with him and the crowd. She later spent almost thirty minutes backstage in Paul's dressing room, enjoying a one-to-one chat with him!

Evguenia (Jane) Enenko has since met Paul several more times and has become a good friend of mine. In May of 2003, I found myself standing next to Jane at the rear of St. Basil's Cathedral in Moscow's Red Square, while waiting to receive my press pack from Geoff Baker just prior to Paul's first-ever Russian gig.

Steve Barnes
Liverpool, England

From Russia With Love: Jane's Story

It started when I was just a teenage girl. One day I fell ill, and my mum didn't let me go to school. So the whole day I was lying on the sofa and watching TV. On one of the channels, I found this black and white movie. The faces of the actors were a bit familiar to me, and moreover, there was nothing to watch on the other channels, so I decided to watch this movie until the end. That was the hour that changed my life. The movie was *A Hard Day's Night!!!!* Since that day, everything has turned over inside of me!!!! After watching it, I had a feeling that for the first fifteen years of my life, my ears had been stuffed up with cotton balls and now somebody had finally pulled them out!

That day I knew my life would never be the same. The Beatles weren't just my favorite band; they also became like a little engine inside of me, making me do thousands of things. All by myself I decided to learn English (in school I was studying French) and in a few years I had entered the State University, the faculty of foreign languages, to learn English. I couldn't imagine my life without music so I started playing in a band. Then last year a very well-known Russian musician and I recorded a CD called "Hello, Paul." (One copy is now in The Beatles Story museum.)

Now I am finishing my studies at the University; I work as a TV presenter for music television; I have my own page ("culture/music") in the biggest newspaper here; and I play in the band. Thank you, John, Paul, George and Ringo!

Of course, from the beginning, my biggest dream was to see three of the Beatles and to visit, even for one day, their native city, Liverpool...but for a long time it was only a dream – the Beatles will never go to Russia and I could never go to the UK (almost impossible to get a visa and find so much money).

But in 2001, thanks to a huge miracle, I was standing on Mathew Street in Liverpool!!!!! I had told my mother I was going to visit friends in Moscow for three weeks. I got a visa by saying I was on a working students' programme. I took a back pack and sleeping bag and went to the UK by walking and hitchhiking all the way. It was a really crazy story and was on the front pages of UK and Russian newspapers!! My story even appeared in the London *Sunday Times*. Honestly, I thought that arriving in Liverpool was the culminating point of my life! But then I found out it was only the beginning!!!!!

That day, in a Liverpool shop, I heard that Paul would be reading his poems at a poetry event somewhere in Wales! Wow! A very small one, but a chance to *see* him! So without any money, without knowing the name of the town (just "somewhere in Wales"), my first time being in this foreign country, and without even knowing the date of this poetry week, I went there by hitchhiking. On my way, I found out the exact location of this poetry week – Hay-on-Wye – and the main thing – Paul will really be there!!!! But all the tickets were sold months ago. Again, by the biggest miracle, I got inside!!!! It is impossible to describe my feelings when I saw HIM...

At the end of the performance they said Paul will answer a few questions from the audience. There was a huge box containing a thousand pieces of paper with questions. He pulled out three pieces of paper...and the second one was mine!!!! And it had happened that earlier somebody told him the story of the adventures of a girl from Russia. So Paul invites me on the stage, gives me a huge hug, and we are reading his poems...together!!!! I thought I would die of happiness!!

Half a year later in London, I had my second meeting with Paul!!!! It happened during another poetry reading in Queen's Theatre in London. And again it was a miracle because Paul recognized me! He recognized me HALF A

YEAR after that meeting in Hay-on-Wye! Taking into account that every day he meets hundreds of people, it was shocking that he even remembered me. That day we were talking like old friends. He was asking me about Russia, about my home city, about Russian people...

Two years after that, Paul gave his FIRST-EVER concert in Russia – 24 May 2003 in Red Square. I was in the first row.

Jane (Evguenia) Enenko, (aka Beatle Jane), Age 24
Cheliabinsk, Russia

From Brazil With Love: Célia's Story

This happened to me just like in a fairy tale...

During my first trip to Liverpool in July 2002, I dropped by the "From Me To You" shop, where I met Steve. We became friends immediately and I even went with him to a photo session for the Blue Meanies (a Beatles cover band from Liverpool).

I already had a ticket for the 16.00 train to London for the next day. But Steve convinced me to stay: "Paul is coming to Liverpool!" I thought, what the hell, maybe I could see Sir Paul McCartney. But I never really imagined that I would shake hands or talk to him.

The following day, the Queen, Paul McCartney and Yoko Ono were all in town. I was standing in "From Me To You" when Beatle Jane walked in. Steve told me that if I went with Jane at once, we might get to see one of them. So I decided to go with Jane. At first, we thought about meeting Paul at the airport (the John Lennon Airport opening) but it didn't work. Instead, we ended up behind the security fences in front of The Walker Gallery, where Paul was going to exhibit his paintings for the Queen.

There were hundreds of policemen keeping us away from Paul. It was eleven o'clock in the morning of 25 July 2002 (oh, sacred day!) when we heard someone say, "That's Paul's Jaguar!!" Then ... it was real! There he was! Paul got out of the car and we started screaming, "Hey, Paul! We travelled so long to see you, please come here!" And he came over!!

I said to him, "Please, Mr. Paul McCartney, I'm from Brazil, could you give me your autograph?" And he was so sweet. "Of course, Brazil, Maracana," he said.

There he was, my idol since I was four years old, standing next to me and giving me his autograph! I could not believe that I was holding the LIPA programme signed by "the Legend." I burst into tears! I ran back to Steve's store at about 70 miles per hour, with tears streaming down my face. I was clutching my LIPA programme signed by Paul.

Definitely, that was the happiest day of my life, and I will always thank Steve and Jane for it ... and the entire Beatles nation, for we are like a brotherhood and sisterhood of tender people who love the music of the Beatles!

Célia Cordeiro da Costa, Age 37
São Paulo, Brazil

Here I am with my signed LIPA programme and a friend!

Célia Cordeiro da Costa, Age 37
São Paulo, Brazil

I Saw Him Standing There

On the evening of 19th December 1999 – after the longest 'rehearsal' in history – Sir Paul McCartney was finally allowed back into the Cavern. And, after passing through the "Lucky Dip" ticket allocation, so was I! Yes, I was one of the fortunate few to receive a ticket. Despite some *very* tempting offers in the local press (£10,000 per ticket) and a grilling from an American TV crew who asked the obvious question: "What would it take to make you give up your ticket?" – to which my reply was, "Lady, give me 5,000 acres of Texas and a face like Brad Pitt and I'll think about it!" – I held on to my ticket.

Everything that can be said has already been said about the gig, so I won't waste your time by repeating it; however, take it from me – it was very, very FAB! Sadly, I had forgotten my camera that night (very unlike me), which would have been removed by the guards at the door anyway, but there were some very naughty people in the rave cave that night who apparently had not forgotten theirs! I managed to borrow one. That was it – I was off snapping like mad till the roll of film was finished. A £10.00 note bought me the film, and the camera was returned to my newest best friend, whom I haven't seen since. If there is ever a prize for photographing dandruff, then that prize is mine, because that is almost all that I achieved.

Despite all that, I was doubly lucky that night because the one good picture I took was of Macca standing right before me…I Saw Him Standing There.

Steve Barnes
Liverpool, England

Liverpool Pays Tribute To George

George Harrison's death was announced at around 8.00 a.m. local time here in the UK. Although we all knew that it would happen, it just didn't seem real. I arrived for work at From Me To You, Cavern Walks, at around 8.30 a.m. to an unreal chill. Understanding that not everyone who works in the mall is a Beatles fan didn't account for the atmosphere. The press and media representatives from around the globe soon arrived. As the MTV had been turned off in the mall, the only sound that could be heard was that of the journalists and their interviewees.

There was obviously an enormous interest from the world's press; however, the news broke just as many locals were beginning their day's work. It was lunchtime before the place began to fill up. People seemed to be finishing work early because they came...and stayed, and that's when the atmosphere began to warm. Margie from Lucy in the Sky Cafe turned up the jukebox playing George songs and people were talking at last. People who looked like they would never stare into a camera lens now stood in line to say their piece, most with tears in their eyes.

We opened our book of condolence in the shop and Eddie Porter, the Magical Mystery Tour guide, was the very first to sign. At this point, all the floral tributes, messages and gifts that were placed on our Beatles statue began to spill over onto the mall, so much so that a local florist was hired to maintain the display. Meanwhile, just a few meters away out on Mathew Street, the John Lennon statue was receiving similar attention: more flowers, more tributes.

People descended the Cavern Club steps to sign their book and later that night, Liverpool's Blue Meanies played a free tribute concert. A book of condolence was opened in the

Town Hall where the flag flew at half mast, just like every other flag around Liverpool.

On Saturday morning people from all around the UK started to arrive many with tales to tell. The one that I will always remember was the young girl from Scotland whom I observed whilst she tearfully signed the book. She thanked George for his hospitality at Friar Park when, as a seriously ill child, she spent time there as the guest of George and his family. The pictures that she produced brought tears to my eyes. There was George with her and both their families in the kitchen, on the grounds, in the hall; very moving.

The week that followed went much the same way. On Monday evening a civic service was held at the city's St. George's Hall, where the book of condolence was made available to a wider audience. Children of the Dovedale Road primary school (George and John's first school) sang *My Sweet Lord* to the crowd of thousands, a song that they only rehearsed that day. The Lord Mayor spoke a tribute. Then the people of Liverpool once again stood in line to pay their respects whilst the world's press watched.

It's not a well-known fact that John and George went to the same school but did not know each other. Some of you may be aware of the significance of the number nine in John Lennon's life. On the calendar, John Lennon and George Harrison passed away *nine* days apart.

Steve Barnes – 2002
Liverpool, England

A Pony Tale

There is a saying that scousers (the good people of Liverpool) get everywhere. It's true.

You may be familiar with a horse race meeting held in Liverpool each year, called the Grand National. It's been run since 1839 and attracts a worldwide audience.

One of the other things that I do is run a small distribution business that mainly consists of taking tourist info to hotels and leisure sites. I was given the contract by the Grand National to distribute publicity material to the rural areas south of Liverpool. These are midlands areas with lots of equine interest. One day recently, I was driving down a country lane near Cheshire, with no idea of where I was. I hadn't seen a person for miles, when, by the side of a canal, I spotted a small shop with adjoining stables. Obviously, these were two worthy delivery points for my cargo. I pulled up and entered the shop first, planning to do the stables second.

I was carrying a large display carton bearing the word, 'Liverpool.' The store was empty, except for the proprietor, a small woman with a smiley face that barely reached past the top of the counter. She spotted the word 'Liverpool' and shouted, "Ah, Liverpool! Lovely Liverpool! I'm from Liverpool!" But hers was not a Liverpool accent.

"Oh, yeah," I said, "From Liverpool, eh? I suppose you knew the Beatles."

"YES!" she said.

I coughed and dropped the box.

She told me her name is Teri Williams and she is in her mid-sixties. Her mum is in her mid-eighties and worked as a secretary to Harry Epstein, Brian's father. Her mum also was a friend of Brian's mum, Queenie Epstein. Teri was employed by Brian Epstein as a 'Saturday Girl' to help out on that one day of the week when N.E.M.S. was at its busiest.

Harry Epstein was a huge racing fan and a great fan of the Grand National. Brian would often buy all the extra racing tickets from him and give them out to the employees.

She tells of one form of training that she received from Brian in order to answer the telephone according to the standard that he required. Teri was told to ring up all the 'posh' stores and businesses in the area to see how they answered the telephone and then do likewise when she took incoming calls.

Brian would bring in visiting American recording artists to do record signings at N.E.M.S. He would invite the American Air Force community based at nearby Burtonwood Airbase to these events in order to make the American artists feel at home. Much to everyone's delight, the American military guys would bring glass bottles of Coca Cola for everyone in the place, a rare treat at the time!

As for the Beatles, Teri says that early on, they often came into the shop to see where their records were placed. Teri describes how they exhibited unabashed delight upon seeing their records for sale. She recalls that all they wanted to do was sing when they came into N.E.M.S.! Sometimes the Beatles would come into the shop and their recordings would be playing. She describes how they just could not stand still and would proceed to literally jump up and down all around the small shop in order to express their glee. Then they'd playfully push and fall on top of one another.

She said that the four lads "oozed enthusiasm and bounced around like they were on elastic." She remembers them being very modest and having no sort of "We're going to be big stars" attitude whatsoever.

She has vivid memories of John bouncing all over the place and yelling, "We've just made a record!" and "Hey, hey, we've done it!" When the four would hear one of their records playing, they'd all jump around and yell, "That's us!! That's us!!"

Steve Barnes – 2004
Liverpool, England

With special thanks to Teri Williams

A Liverpudlian Finds Paul
Back In The USSR

On the evening of May 24th, Sir Paul McCartney finally got 'back' to the USSR. We are told that this was not only his first performance there, but his first visit to Russia. It was the fantastically warm evening of a fine summer's day and the stage was set at the St. Basil's Cathedral end of Red Square just a few hundred meters from Lenin's mausoleum. An expected 20,000 people would witness history being made. This was really Lenin and McCartney!

Russia missed out on Beatlemania when it swept the world in the 1960s as the Beatles were deeply disapproved of in the Soviet Union. The Beatles had been dismissed as "the belch of Western culture," and even as recently as the 1980s, Paul was refused permission to play in Russia. President Putin, now 51, was a teenager during the '60s and said of the Beatles' music at a televised meeting with Paul, "It was very popular, more than popular. It was like a breath of fresh air, like a window on the world. I'm sure a lot of people play and sing your songs. They like you a lot." Tonight was the Moscow fans' chance to catch up.

All surrounding access to the venue was, as you'd expect, sealed and guarded by assorted ranks of military personnel. People had begun queuing at the several access points all day. I arrived at 8 p.m. for the expected 8.30 start and found a comfortable position midway through the crowd, just opposite the middle of the Kremlin buildings.

The crowd was far from the expected 50,000 people. It was more like 20,000, possibly due to the locally high ticket prices of 1,000 rubles to 10,000 rubles ($30 to $320). If any of Paul's concerts should have been free, apart from the Liverpool ones, then this one was it.

The pre-show theatre took place. As soon as a silhouette image of Paul holding the legendary trademark Hofner appeared on a white screen, there he was on stage.

I have been lucky enough to have been at close quarters with Paul on many occasions in Liverpool and have shared that excitement with people from all over the globe, but on that night in Red Square I was proud to be amongst the people of Russia sharing this truly historic event with them. The atmosphere was absolutely magic! It was almost as good as when I saw Paul sing *Yesterday* at George's tribute concert in Liverpool. There were cheers, tears and sighs of disbelief ... fabulous, just fabulous, and I was there!

Banners in the crowd proclaimed in English, "30 years waiting for you!" "Thanks Paul!" and "No War, Just Beatles." There was heavy police and military presence and it seemed that people having fun was unacceptable to some of the officials, as there were reports of some of them confiscating bottles of water and actually ordering people to stop dancing.

He opened his show as usual with *Hello Goodbye* and made good use of the final lyric to welcome the audience. *Lady Madonna, Hey Jude, She's Leaving Home,* and *Getting Better* all followed, along with solo numbers and Wings classics. People danced along, sang along, and cried along with each other. I bet that many new friendships were formed that night.

As you know, this was one of the last gigs of an extensive tour, but Paul was clearly still touched by the powerful outpouring of emotion. "I hear that a lot of you learned to speak English through the Beatles; how does that make me feel?" Translations appeared on the screens whenever Paul spoke and he thanked and mimicked the translator below him, to the amusement of the crowd.

Back in the USSR had the expected effect on the crowd. "Finally we got to do that one here!" said Paul, and the crowd went wild as I expected, but what I did not expect was for him to play it *twice*. Paul explained that this was a request for a very special person. It seems that President Putin was not expected to attend the concert at all, having been treated to Paul's private rendition of *Let It Be* earlier that day inside the Kremlin; however, about thirty minutes into the gig, he and his guests strolled out of the Kremlin and sat down between Moscow's Mayor Yury Luzhkov and Russian rock star Andrei Makarevich. Having missed the first rendition of *Back in the USSR*, President Putin was the special person for whom Paul sang it a second time.

Paul commented before the concert that he had known very little about the Soviet Union when he wrote the song. "It was a mystical land then," he said. "It's nice to see the reality. I always suspected that people here had big hearts. Now I know that's true."

Paul's tribute to John was extremely moving. He told the audience, "Every opportunity to tell friends and loved ones what you think of them should be taken whilst you can, no matter how embarrassed or uncomfortable you may feel." He then played *Here Today*. George came next, with Paul performing his ukulele version of *Something*, in moving tribute to his mate.

And so, after two and a half hours, 20,000 happy people and a very happy me left Red Square, passing through what seemed to be an almost equal number of less fortunate fans stationed outside around the perimeter. Such a shame, as inside there certainly was room for more. Maybe next time...

Steve Barnes, May 2003
With thanks to Eugenia Tenneco and Julia Gregory

Every Head He's Had the Pleasure to Know

Recently I was showing some of our guests a map of places to see in and around Penny Lane. When I finished, a man whom I had noticed paying attention in the background walked over and asked to see the map.

He took the map and placed his finger on the barber shop at No. 7 Smithdown Place. "I worked there," he said.

Les Manu, now aged 69, worked at Bioletti's Barbers located at the rear of the bus shelter at the centre of the Penny Lane intersection, beginning in 1957. He remembers both John and Paul coming to the barber shop (separately) before they were famous, and he would cut their pre-Beatle hair. Les recalls that, a few years later, John would have a haircut and then wait there for Cynthia Powell, who worked at the nearby Woolworth store on Allerton Road.

Les explains that he used to visit both the Strawberry Fields orphanage and the Bluecoat School, another Liverpool orphanage at the time, to cut the children's hair. Harry Bioletti, the owner of Bioletti's, had contracts to provide all the haircuts at both these places. Les specialized in cutting boys' hair, so he went to both orphanages on a regular basis.

Whenever I describe the Penny Lane experience to our guests, I tell them this. As a kid, Paul used to ride the bus from his home in Allerton to school (the Liverpool Institute). This route would take him past a fire station near the end of Rose Lane. Going onward, the bus would pass the shelter located at the intersection of Allerton Road, Smithdown Road, Church Road and Penny Lane.

A bank, a barber, and a pretty nurse selling poppies might all have been observed by Paul. There may well have been, on occasion, blue suburban skies. We know for sure that Paul had then (and still does) eyes and ears (and, boy, has he made good use of them!!)

So, it was pure observation mixed with genius, good timing, and maybe a little luck thrown in! Paul McCartney put the whole lot on the world map, forever attaching a Beatle connection to each of these locations.

I believe that there may have been an even earlier Beatle connection. When John's father, Freddie Lennon, was about seven, his dad died. Freddie's mother was left with six children and no money. She was forced to accept the offer of places for two of her children at the Bluecoat orphanage. Freddie Lennon and his sister, Edith, were dispatched there.

If visiting the Bluecoat School to cut the children's hair was a Bioletti's tradition, then there's a fair chance that the Lennon association with Bioletti's barbershop was, in fact, its earliest and little-known Beatles connection.

Steve Barnes
Liverpool, England

The Cavern Club – Facts and Fiction

"The place was a claustrophobic hell, but it was a great hell!"

– Paul McCartney

Stuck down a back street in an old, decrepit warehouse, the Cavern was hot, sweaty and stank of disinfectant. The setting was unpromising but to those who descended the narrow steps into the basement it was the centre of the universe...for *here,* a music revolution was taking place.

The Cavern began life as a stronghold for jazz, with some of the artists coming from as far away as London. Frustrated by the lack of opportunities to play in City Centre locations, the Beatles and other local musicians would approach the club manager, Ray McFall, asking for dates to play, but they were refused for months.

"Can we work here?"

"No, it's a jazz club and we don't want Rock n' Roll here, it's crap!" he'd say, but the bands persisted. Finally he agreed to try Rock n' Roll at the lunchtime sessions, to try to appeal to the young workers who popped in for a soup, cheese roll and a soft drink.

The Cavern Club - Facts & Fiction!

Myth One: The Cavern was knocked down in 1973 and in its place a car park was built.

The Facts: The Cavern Club was, and still is, a basement cellar club. The buildings above the Cavern were fruit warehouses. These were knocked down in 1973. The Cavern was below ground level; thus it was not knocked down, it was simply filled in.

The Reason for the Myth: When the fruit warehouses were knocked down, it left an open space within the City Centre. This open ground was used by the locals as a car parking space. A car park was never built, as the mythology would have you believe.

Myth Two: The original Cavern was on the opposite side of the road from the Cavern Club today.

The Facts: The Cavern today occupies 50% of its original site. The address of the Cavern when it opened in 1957 was 10 Mathew Street. The address is still 10 Mathew Street today.

The Reason for the Myth: The fruit warehouses above the Cavern were demolished in 1973 and the Cavern Club closed down. The Council was planning to use the Cavern basements for improvements to the Merseyside Underground Railway system (which never did materialise). The Cavern Club was filled in and remained so until 1982.

Meanwhile, the owner of the Cavern, Mr. Roy Adams, opened a new club opposite the original site, calling it the Cavern. He erected a new 30-foot Cavern sign over the new doorway and an accompanying plaque which stated, "The Cavern Club today now stands opposite from the original site." In 1973 this sign was relevant and the information on the plaque was correct.

In 1974, the new Cavern Club folded. Roy Adams launched the club again as the Revolution, which also folded. Eventually, success was found on this site with the launch of yet another venue, Eric's, which gained a worldwide reputation during the punk rock revolution. Sadly, when punk died, so did Eric's.

Throughout the Revolution and Eric's era, the 30-foot Cavern sign remained, as did the plaque. Indeed, both remained until 1992, when severe winter gales finally blew the sign down, nearly 20 years after it was originally erected.

In December 1980 John Lennon was murdered. Local architect David Blackhouse won approval for plans to reopen the original Cavern, which remained intact underground. He envisaged the reopening and redevelopment of the area as a lasting tribute to John. In late 1981, the Cavern was knocked down. The original bricks were saved, treated and utilised in the rebuilding of the Cavern on its original site to its original dimensions. In 1984 the Cavern Club reopened on its original site. The timetable of events is irrefutable, so why is there any confusion? Quite simply, Roy Adams's sign and plaque remained in position from 1973-1992. When the Cavern reopened on its original site, many locals believed the 30-foot sign and plaque on the opposite side of the street were indicators of the site of the original Cavern Club. This, of course, is absurd. From 1984-1992 this sign was not relevant and the information on the plaque was incorrect.

Myth Three: Next to the Cavern Club is a car park (open space). Below that car park are remains from the original club.

The Facts: There is indeed a car park next to the Cavern Club now. David Blackhouse can confirm that all this area under the car park was filled in. There are no remains of the original club directly under the car park.

The Reason for the Myth: This appears to be a combination of the two myths: that the club was knocked down for a car park and that the site of the present Cavern Club is not the site of the original. The fact remains that the Cavern today occupies 50% of its original site.

Conclusion

There has been a Cavern Club on the site of 10 Mathew Street for 40 years. The Cavern Club closed from 1973-1984. The original club was knocked down in 1982 as the site was excavated and although the club was intact, the foundations were unsafe.

The bricks of the Club were saved and treated and used in the building of the Cavern Club, which stands today. The original Cavern plans were used to reconstruct today's Cavern. The arches, dimensions and the floor space in the front of the club are more or less exact to the original club. There are three major differences:

1. The club today only occupies 50% of the original site.

2. The club is, in fact, deeper than the original club. In 1962 you would have to descend 18 stairs; today you will descend 30 steps.

3. When you entered the Cavern basement, the stage was directly in front of you. Today the stage is to the left.

Steve Barnes
Liverpool, England

A Special Note of Thanks

I wish to acknowledge Steve Barnes of Liverpool for the stories that appear on pages 196-218, and thank him for his advice and support.

I didn't know Steve at all when I e-mailed him with a question in November 2003. He took an immediate interest in this project and has gone out of his way to be helpful in a bunch of ways. Steve asked for (and received) nothing in return. He simply went out of his way for a fellow Beatles fan. I truly thank him for his generous spirit, his enthusiasm for this book, and for sharing his vast Beatles knowledge. Steve is a wonderful resource for any visitor to Liverpool.

Steve can be contacted at From Me To You, Upper Level, Cavern Walks Shopping Mall, Mathew Street, Beatle Village, Liverpool L2 6RE. The store features a large range of fully licensed Beatles merchandise. They also offer a "Beatle Wonderland" information service, free maps of Beatle Village and the Penny Lane vicinity, a free-of-charge "bag-park" (subject to space availability), and the warmest welcome you'll find anywhere.

Steve's e-mail address is: liverpoolaccent@yahoo.co.uk

Web site: www.beatles64.co.uk

~ LS

About the Editor

Linda Schultz lives in a suburb of Boston, Massachusetts. She is currently a research administrator at a university and does free-lance writing as a hobby. Her articles about the Beatles have appeared in *Good Day Sunshine* and the British monthly publication, *The Beatles Book*. She has been a Beatles fan since day one and is proud of the fact that she raised her two children to be avid Beatle fans. Getting to meet Paul McCartney in person at his June 2001 book signing in New York City is the single most thrilling thing that has ever happened to her...so far, anyway.